THIS MEAN DISEASE

Growing Up in the Shadow
of My Mother's Anorexia Nervosa

DANIEL BECKER

FOREWORD BY JOEL YAGER, MD

gürze books

This Mean Disease
Growing up in the Shadow of My Mother's Anorexia Nervosa
© 2005 by Daniel Becker

Gürze Books
P.O. Box 2238
Carlsbad, CA 92018
800-756-7533
www.bulimia.com

Cover design by Johnson Design
Cover photo © Getty Images, Rights-managed collection

Lyrics to "Casey Jones" and "Ripple" by Robert Hunter
© Ice Nine Publishing Company. Used with permission.
Lyrics to "Goodbye Yellow Brick Road by Elton John & Bernie Taupin
© Universal Music Group. Used with permission.

Library of Congress Cataloging-in-Publication Data

Becker, Daniel, 1962-
This mean disease : growing up in the shadow of my mother's anorexia nervosa / Daniel Becker ; foreward by Joel Yager.
    p. cm.
ISBN 10: 0-936077-50-6 (alk. paper)
ISBN 13: 978-0-936077-50-5
 1. Becker, Daniel, 1962- 2. Becker, Carol Oberman--Health. 3. Anorexia nervosa--Patients--United States--Biography. 4. Anorexia nervosa--Patients--United States--Family relationships. 5. Mothers and sons--United States--Biography. I. Title.
RC552.A5B43 2005
616.85'262'0092--dc22   2005015876

NOTE
The author and publisher of this book intend for this publication to provide accurate information. It is sold with the understanding that it is meant to complement, not substitute for, professional medical and/or psychological services.

All of the events and persons in this book are real. However, some names have been changed to protect their privacy.

2 4 6 8 0 9 7 5 3 1

THIS MEAN DISEASE

PROLOGUE

Mom's ashes are surprisingly heavy. Is it possible that they could weigh more than she did when she died? After almost 30 years of anorexia nervosa, the cumulative effects are contained in a white porcelain urn.

My two brothers and sister-in-law—Jimmy, John, and Sandra—are with me as we prepare to offer Mom's ashes to the Pacific Ocean. We are onboard the Naiad, the Neptune Society's yacht, which has just puttered under the arching span of the Golden Gate

Bridge. A strong April wind blows, causing the four of us to rise and fall with the swell.

The engine stops. The priest, in his black shirt and white collar, murmurs that it is time to begin the service. The woman at the Neptune Society assured us that he is capable of performing a Jewish ceremony. Sure enough, he hands each of us a Xerox copy of the Kaddish, the Jewish prayer for the dead. The page contains no Hebrew, only a transliteration: "Yitgadal, veyitgadash, ve shmay raba…" He also gives me the white porcelain urn.

Stepping out on deck I gaze at the brown hills of the Marin headlands, which remind me of giant camels at rest. My brothers and I recite the Kaddish, struggling to be heard over the wind as we take turns pouring ashes into our hands, then tipping them over the rail and into the water.

When it is my turn, I am surprised by the coarseness of the ash. I had expected a fine white powder, like sand on a Caribbean beach. This is more like residue from a barbecue pit.

"You're losing her," my brothers cry, as a gust of wind blows the ashes back on the boat. After a brief hesitation, we chuckle, then laugh. We remember that we are here, on this boat, in the middle of the San Francisco Bay, to venerate Mom's spirit, not her body. For a moment, we forget the many years she was unwilling or unable to nourish that body, and the helplessness we felt watching her slowly fade away.

When all the ash is disbursed, the Naiad's engines rumble to life and the boat makes a lazy turn back toward the Bridge and the San Francisco city beyond. I take a last look at the patch of water where the ashes are scattered. It is already indistinguishable from the rest of the green expanse.

1

DEPARTURE

Because I have no specific recollections, I have had to piece together the start of Mom's anorexia nervosa like an archeologist digging for answers. What I know is that the disorder first manifested itself in 1965, the summer when Mom's parents, Irving and Isabel Oberman, vacationed with our family at Lake Tahoe.

Mom wanted to lose ten pounds before wearing a bathing suit. A decade later, she described the onset in a *San Francisco Chronicle* interview:

> I went off to Lake Tahoe one summer. I was a little bit
> overweight—I weighed about 135 pounds—and I wanted
> to look good in a bathing suit. I thought I'd lose about
> ten pounds. I lost the ten, but then I never stopped los-
> ing—down to 120, then 115, then 112, then 85 pounds.
> I was quite emotionally disturbed at that time. It wasn't
> that I was never hungry. I wouldn't let myself eat.

Anorexia nervosa is often triggered by some kind of traumatic emotional experience. Dr. JoEllen Werne, a psychiatrist who has treated many anorexia patients, including Mom, has described a typical onset in this way: "an adolescent, almost always a girl from an intact middle-class family, embarks on a project that is quite concrete—to lose a few pounds—often spurred on by some disappointment in friendship or a stressful life event. This idea of self-improvement soon becomes lost in the pursuit of thinness for its own sake."[1]

Mom differed from Dr. Werne's description in one important respect: She began her diet not in adolescence, but at the age of 34, with a husband and three young children.

~

I had a special bond with Carol Oberman Becker that began the night of my birth. On February 27, 1962, my soon-to-be mother, nine months pregnant, had awakened in a pool of blood. The telephone call jolted Dr. John Kerner, our family's obstetrician, from his sleep. Dr. Kerner immediately ordered an ambulance, threw on some clothes, and ran the two blocks to our house. It must have been a terrible surprise considering how uneventful the pregnancy had been, as well as the normal births of my two older brothers.

The ambulance was in our driveway by the time Dr. Kerner arrived. So were some of the neighbors, in bathrobes and slippers, drawn by the siren and the revolving red light flashing across the house's white clapboard. When the neighbors saw Mom carried out on a stretcher, followed anxiously by Dad, they surely guessed it had to do with the pregnancy. They would have seen her recently at Julius Kahn playground, resting her large belly on a bench while her two young sons played on the monkey bars and merry-go-round. Maybe she had even shared with some of them her secret hope that this time she would give birth to a girl, an ally in a house full of men. Perhaps I, the third son deep in the womb, jealous of her desire, decided to cause some trouble.

Of all people, the neighbors must have thought, Carol Becker was the least likely to have something go awry with her pregnancy. She was a robust woman, big-boned and tall. "A Viking goddess," as one friend described, referring not only to her physique but to her red-blonde hair and pale, almost translucent skin.

At the hospital, Dr, Kerner induced labor, and I was delivered normally. The only evidence of my hurried arrival was the *Baby Boy Becker* typed where the name should have been on my birth certificate. Subsequently, I was thrilled to hear Mom and Dad describe the adventure of my birth.

Dr. Kerner later told me the medical term for my mother's condition: "It was premature separation of the normally-implanted placenta," he said. Separation had been there from the start.

~

A family photograph taken when I was three months old shows me sitting on Mom's lap, a smiling, fat baby in a white jumper. The picture confirms something I have been told, yet still find so difficult to believe: At that time, there was no hint of anything unusual about our family.

Mom and I are part of a circle that includes Dad, my two older brothers Jimmy and John, and Dad's parents, Grandma and Grandpa B. Mom holds me in both arms, her eyes scrunched up and her mouth displaying a row of even, white teeth. A few lines extend from her eyes, nothing unusual for a 32-year-old woman with three young children. Dad perches over us, suited in coat and tie, his short, combed black hair already shot through with gray. John reaches out to touch my hand, while Jimmy, also looking at me, has the slightest hint of mischief in his smile.

This is the moment where, if I could, I would stop time. Despite my early arrival, I am haunted by the idea that I came along just a little too late. Too late to know who my mother really was, too late to see her shine. Maybe I hurried from the womb to drink in more of those precious days before Mom's anorexia nervosa robbed a part of her from me forever.

"We used to call her the golden girl," one family friend said. "She had it all." Another used to call her "Champagne Charlie, because she just sparkled." This is the person I wish I could remember.

Instead, in my earliest memory, I am three years old and gazing up at a suitcase that juts over the side of my parents' bed. It is Mom's suitcase and she slowly fills it with shoes, blouses, and dresses. We are in the master bedroom of our quaint, French country-style house on 135 Locust Street in San Francisco. Jimmy and John are also in the room, and they must be standing because they are looming over me. The three of us are subdued, our attention fixed on the suitcase as if it holds some precious truth about the future.

From my perspective as a little boy, there is nothing unusual about Mom's appearance, though she must have looked deathly. She weighed only 74 pounds—which seems like an impossibility—on her five-foot-eight-inch frame. Her psychiatrist at the Menninger

Foundation, who would see her for the first time a few days later, said that she reminded him of "an Auschwitz survivor, one of those Holocaust victims from World War II."

That moment in the bedroom is the only image I retain from Mom's first departure. I don't recall her closing the bag, or Dad carrying it downstairs and out the front door to his waiting Ford Thunderbird. I don't recall whether she was crying, or held me for an extra long time, or told me to be brave and that she would return soon. I don't recall whether I could feel the sharp poke of her bones when we hugged goodbye.

~

"My mother used to tell us what we could and couldn't eat," Mom often said. "She hovered over my sister and I to make sure we finished everything on our plates. If we didn't, there would be hell to pay. I hated it and promised myself I would never do that to you guys."

Even though Grandma Oberman died when I was ten, I can still picture her pinched face and feel a foreboding, like the beginning of a scary movie, her presence evoked. This feeling was enhanced by her most prominent feature—a hand tremor. Mom told me to ignore it, but whenever Isabel lifted a spoonful of soup to her mouth, I couldn't help staring to see if the broth would reach her lips or wind up splashed on the tablecloth. She used those same shaky hands to spoon out the ice from Grandpa Oberman's water glass whenever we went out to dinner. "The ice isn't good for him," she'd say as her husband sat silently beside her.

The hands hadn't always been shaky. In an autobiographical statement Mom typed during one of her hospitalizations, she wrote that Isabel had ruled their house "with an iron fist."

The need to control was high on my grandmother's list. Everything from the food Mom ate to the friends she had were under Isabel's strict authority. Listening in on phone conversations and preventing Mom from inviting friends over to the house were typical behaviors. Isabel was so obsessed with Mom's health, she even examined her bowel movements.

Mom's older sister, Joyce, agrees that Isabel was overbearing, but points to one big difference between Mom's attitude and her own. "I just turned the other cheek," Joyce says, "but your mother used to stew about it. 'It's not fair,' she would say. I tried to tell her to let it go, but she couldn't." Mom was a good girl, much too well-behaved to confront her parents directly.

Only long after Isabel's death did I realize that no portrait of her had ever hung on the wall among the family photographs. And Mom never spoke her name, except on those occasions when John, a notoriously picky eater, refused to finish his vegetables. "No dessert for you," Jimmy and I would tease. Mom would quickly interrupt us with an uncharacteristic seriousness. "He doesn't have to finish his main course to have dessert. I'm not your Grandma Oberman."

During the family vacation to Lake Tahoe, Isabel buried Mom under an avalanche of criticism. She probably objected to the food Mom prepared for us. For breakfast, we craved crispy bacon on white toast with a generous slathering of butter. For lunch, we preferred bologna sandwiches dotted with gobs of mayonnaise. Isabel, a follower of Gaylord Hauser, an early vitamin proponent, was probably critiquing everything we put in our mouths. It must have pained Mom, now an adult with children of her own, to find herself being treated with the same insignificance as when she was a child.

She turned to her father. "Help me Daddy," she pleaded.

In contrast to Isabel, Irving had a warm and inviting presence, and his portrait had always assumed a prominent place on the wall. Short and stout, with straw-colored hair and rosy cheeks, his friends were inspired to nickname him "Ike the Swedish Jew." We simply called him "Grandpa O." Whenever he visited, my brothers and I vied to have him walk us around the living room on his shiny, black shoes. Mom loved to tell stories about him, particularly his propensity to deliver painful puns.

Each year, on the anniversary of his death, when she was not away in a hospital somewhere, Mom would invite my brothers and me to accompany her to the Friday night memorial service at Temple Emanuel. At the service, the rabbi read aloud the names of those people whose death anniversaries had occurred during the previous week. When "Irving Oberman" was said aloud, Mom would squeeze the hand of whichever of us was sitting next to her and snuffle into her handkerchief in the temple's dim light.

Despite his sense of humor, Irving was no pushover. He was the only one of his eight brothers and sisters to attend college, Harvard no less. He started his own textile business. After one of his brothers asked for money, he broke off all communication with him. Similarly, he stopped speaking to his brother-in-law, Mom's beloved Uncle Harry, after Harry tried to discuss business during a Passover seder. Perhaps it was from Grandpa O. that Mom inherited the iron will she would later focus on not eating.

But nobody, not even Irving, could stand up to Isabel. At that critical moment, on the shores of icy Lake Tahoe, when Mom asked her father for help in combating her mother's unceasing criticism, Irving merely shrugged his shoulders.

"I'm sorry dear," he told her. "There's nothing I can do."

None of the men in her life—neither her father, nor her husband, nor certainly her three young children—rescued Mom from
Isabel. I imagine, at that moment, a little piece of glass entering
Mom's heart, like the splintered mirror fragment that freezes Kay's
heart in Hans Christian Andersen's *The Snow Queen*. I know, of course,
that no single event triggers such a baffling and complex illness as
anorexia nervosa. But that doesn't prevent me from wishing that I
had been older and able to tell Isabel that Mom was doing a fine job,
that we wouldn't have changed a thing about her, that we adored
her. I wish it even if it is a fantasy.

Growing up in Woodmere, on New York's Long Island, Mom's
childhood was filled with accomplishments. At her parent's insistence,
she took piano lessons and played beautifully. She was a good athlete,
particularly in tennis, and an excellent student, having graduated
from Wellesley College. At 24, she married my father, a nice Jewish
boy from a good family who had attended the right schools: Horace
Mann, Dartmouth College, Harvard Business School. The two in-
law families, the Beckers and the Obermans, got along wonderfully.
All seemed perfect.

Irving and Isabel had always lived close to Mom. After Wellesley, when Mom took a job in New York City, they decided to leave
Woodmere and move into the City themselves. So I'm sure it was
cataclysmic to them when, in 1957, Mom and Dad announced they
were moving all the way across the country.

Dad had received a job offer to co-own a shoe business in the
San Francisco Bay area. A change in scenery sounded exciting to
Mom, who told Dad she was delighted to go. But Irving and Isabel,
who previously treated Dad as the son they never had, were furious.

Mom, faced with the withering displeasure of her parents and scared to stand up to them, lied that she didn't want to go. Telling that lie must have left her with a deep hole of guilt.

By 1965, something had fractured. Maybe it was Mom's unexpressed anger toward Isabel, which continued to fester. Maybe it was guilt from the move to San Francisco or the stress of raising three young children. Maybe it was that my father, handsome and educated though he was, also turned out to be taciturn, a difficult man to read for approval. Outwardly, none of these things could be detected in Mom's demeanor. Inside, though, something had darkened, like a candle losing its glow.

After the family returned to San Francisco from Lake Tahoe and Irving and Isabel went back to New York, Mom continued to lose weight. She had many excuses for why it was happening. Our house had recently been gutted by plumbers, which resulted in damage to the roof and flooding in one of the closets. The anxiety cost Mom a few pounds. Then she came down with the flu, which cost her a few more. Soon she weighed only 90 pounds.

At the same time, Mom began to demonstrate some of the tricks she later grew to master in her nearly 30 years of anorexia nervosa: rearranging the food on her dinner plate to leave the impression she had eaten, wearing oversized clothes to hide her diminishing figure.

Nobody knew what to do. Back in those days, anorexia nervosa was still a rare disease. Dr. Kerner, who was also Mom's gynecologist, noticed her declining weight and gently suggested she consult with Dr. Walker, the head of Mount Zion Hospital's Psychiatric Department and considered to be one of the best psychiatrists in San Francisco. Prior to his appointment at Mount Zion, Dr. Walker had held a high position at the Menninger Foundation, a world-renowned psychiatric clinic in Topeka, Kansas.

Mom entered psychoanalysis with Dr. Walker, but her weight continued to decline. Her friend Beverly Gasner, whom Mom and Dad visited in Puerto Rico around this time, described her shock in seeing how Mom had changed. "She still had a beautiful face," Beverly recalled, "but she looked like a waif. She had come to visit me because I was in the hospital, and all I could think about was that I needed to get out of bed so she could lie down."

In her diminished state, Mom contracted pneumonia and wound up in her own hospital bed. Her doctors, desperate to get her to eat something, anything, injected her with insulin to induce hypoglycemia and make her crave sugar. On the bedside table, within easy reach, they placed a glass of orange juice. Dad watched silently as Mom, despite her body's convulsions, refused to touch the glass.

Her weight dipped below 80 pounds. The doctors began to whisper about death. Dr. Walker placed a telephone call to the Menninger Foundation. "I have a woman here in San Francisco who needs your help," he told them. "You are her only chance."

The call ignited a debate at Menninger. In 1965, there wasn't a single anorexia nervosa patient at the clinic. The disease was so rare, in fact, that the staff at Menninger weren't sure they would be able to handle Mom. Some of the psychiatrists worried they lacked the regular hospital facilities necessary to ensure her safety. Others expressed sympathy for her plight and the belief that Menninger was her last and only hope. Perhaps, in the end, it was Dr. Walker's influence that convinced them. In the late fall of 1965, they allowed Mom to come to Topeka.

~

Almost 40 years later, I piloted a rental car 90 miles to Topeka from the closest airport in Kansas City. Driving across the snow-dappled

Kansas prairie, I imagined Mom and Dad making the same trip for the first time in late 1965. Topeka is on the eastern edge of the Flint Hills, high prairie country. The landscape, dotted with barns and grain silos, stretches on for 600 unchanging miles until halted by the abrupt uplift of the Rockies. Kansans are said to make good sailors; they are comfortable looking out day after day over a limitless horizon.

When I ask Dad about that car trip, he removes his glasses and looks down at the ground. His voice grows tight. "It was terrible," he says, shaking his head. "Here I was taking your mother 2,000 miles from home, away from her husband and children. She didn't know a soul there. She was scared and so was I. More than anything, it was just so sad." His voice tapers off.

I never had the chance to ask Mom about it, but when I mention the incident to women friends their responses are always the same. "She must have felt so guilty leaving her children like that. That has to be the worst thing a mother can experience."

When Mom and Dad approached Topeka, they saw the state Capitol dome rising above the plains. Another sign, the "World Psychiatric Center" was their real welcome. As they pulled off the highway at Sixth and Gage on the pastoral, western side of town, they glimpsed the Menninger campus for the first time—20 acres of brick and wooden buildings, many of them old farm structures, surrounded by landscaped grounds.

This was one of the first private psychiatric clinics in the country, opening in 1925. Perhaps Mom, gazing out at the rural landscape, was thinking more about the serene Wellesley campus or Camp Vega, on the shores of Maine's Echo Lake, where she passed many summers as a young girl.

As they entered the main administrative building, a white-shingled farmhouse, they noticed behind it the brick, two-story C.F. Menninger Memorial Hospital, Mom's new home. It looked bright and airy, with plenty of windows. Mom would not yet know that the drapes in those windows sat in undersized brackets so they would collapse if a patient tried to use them to hang themselves. Or that the mosquito screens outside the windows were bolted into place to prevent escape. Or that the electrical outlets were placed far from the sinks to deter electrocution. Mom would not yet know that once she entered the hospital, she would not be allowed outside again for six months.

As Dr. Jacobs, the psychiatrist assigned to Mom's case, explained to Dad: "If your wife so much as catches a cold, we're afraid she might die."

This was the first of several shocks Dad received. Before departing Topeka, Dad met with Dr. Jacobs, a native North Carolinian with a soft accent and deep blue eyes that resembled Mom's.

"What do I do now?" he asked Dr. Jacobs.

"Go back to San Francisco and do not contact your wife for six months. A social worker will be in touch about her progress."

"When will she be able to come home?"

"We can't predict," Dr. Jacobs said. "To be honest, I can't say whether you will ever see her again."

As Dad later recalls, "I thought I was bringing her there to get better, not to die."

I cannot imagine this goodbye between my parents who, just a few months earlier, were amidst the ups and downs of a normal life. I still wonder what was really going on in Mom's mind, with three children desperately needing her attention and a husband willing to do anything to help her get better. Perhaps she watched my father's car pull away, wishing she could run to the passenger door and jump inside. More likely, she was probably relieved to be free of the responsibilities that she could no longer handle.

No one had any answers.

2

FAIRY TALE

Young animals, when suddenly removed from their mothers, will often cry continuously and then slip into a state of prolonged lethargy. What happened to me was a different story.

As memories of Mom faded and I could no longer recall what she smelled like or the sound of her voice or how it felt to bounce on her lap or snuggle in her arms, she became less real and more mythical. Because I could not visualize where she was, I constructed an imagined setting where I pictured her locked up, like a lonely princess in a fairy tale. What was around me every day was real; Mom and Menninger slowly grew into a legend.

Six months after Mom's hospitalization began, I had already aligned myself with a substitute caregiver, Helen Frank, our black housekeeper from Opelousas, Louisiana. My parents had hired Helen just before I was born and after Mom's departure, my father placed her in charge of child rearing. Helen, who had already raised two daughters as a single mother, accepted the added responsibility. "No problem," she told Dad, "I'll teach those kids good."

I attached myself to Helen, as if by an invisible rope and trailed her around the house assisting with chores. Enchanted by the blue shade of Ajax powder against white tiles, I helped her scrub the bathtubs. While she reattached buttons to Dad's shirts or stitched name tags on our underwear, I sat alongside and popped needles in and out of her red velvet sewing ball the size of a Christmas ornament.

In Mom's absence, Helen filled the house with her presence. Her mouth was always in motion: talking on the telephone for hours, chewing a toothpick, smoking a Pall Mall cigarette or, most often, grumbling to herself. Helen's southern roots were exposed in her aphorisms. Dad was always "your daddy." We never exited the car; instead we "hopped out like mustard seeds." Her response to our "see you tomorrow" never varied: "God spare life."

It would have been natural to turn to Dad instead, but he wasn't home much. Six days a week he worked downtown, running the shoe concession he owned at the Joseph Magnin department store chain. Occasionally, Helen brought my brothers and I downtown for a visit. We rode the elevator to his office and prowled around, curious to understand what he did all day. Sometimes, he walked us the few blocks to the store where I watched the sales people coddle the ladies' feet. To me, buying shoes was almost as big a waste of time as trying on clothes at Young Man's Fancy or getting a haircut.

Dad always wore a coat and tie. Sometimes, I even imagined that he slept in a suit. Years later, when he was in his 70s, I found him in a pair of blue jeans and remarked that I had never seen him wearing denim before. "These are my first pair," he said. I mostly saw Dad at dinnertime where he tried to maintain some kind of order. Most nights, he checked our fingernails before we sat down. If they were too dirty, he dispatched us to the bathroom to clean them up. He kept the dinner table rules: no leaning back in your chair, no singing, no yelling.

He must have been barely hanging on. For those first months that Mom was at Menninger, the only reports came from a social worker who was part of the treatment team. And since Mom was not allowed outside the hospital, the reports were sparse. Dad learned that Mom was taking meals in her room, attended by a nurse who sat patiently until all the food had been consumed, no matter how long it took. He heard that Mom was having trouble with digestion and that the nurse kept a bottle of air freshener close by for obvious reasons. Dr. Jacobs met with her every day, but Dad had no idea what was discussed.

Sometimes I try to put myself in Dad's shoes. Nothing in his experience had prepared him to be a single father. His own father worked long hours away from home. Murry Becker, or Grandpa B. as we called him, was a successful attorney who had founded his own firm in New York City. He was charismatic but stern, the kind of man who closely intertwined love with respect. As a child, though I was always excited to see him, I could never quite shake my fear of his disapproval.

Grandpa B. would have been a difficult man to live up to, a man whose study was lined with plaques of recognition. In his career he cast a long shadow; as a father he didn't provide Dad with much guidance.

~

Despite all that he did not know, Dad could at least take solace that Mom was in what was generally considered the best psychiatric hospital in the nation.

The Menninger Clinic was a world away from the state-run mental hospitals that had dominated psychiatric practice in the early twentieth century. If Mom had been placed in one of those facilities, it is possible she would have spent the remainder of her life institutionalized.

For so-called new psychiatrists of this era, including Karl Menninger, the Holy Grail was a mental hospital where doctors could focus on research, teaching, and ultimately, the cure of mental illness. In 1925, Karl and his father purchased a 20-acre farm on the western edge of Topeka and converted the farmhouse into a 12-bed sanitarium with administrative offices on the ground floor. As the clinic's reputation grew and referrals came in from other hospitals, additional beds were created through the renovation of existing farm buildings and construction of new facilities.

By the time Mom was admitted, the Menninger Clinic had achieved national and international fame. A large children's division was created, along with the Menninger School of Psychiatry and a research division. The hospital had grown to include 150 inpatient beds and another 34 slots for an outpatient hospital program. But even with the size of the hospital, anorexia nervosa was such a rare illness that none of the doctors had any expertise with it. For the staff at Menninger, Mom would be a test case.

~

After six months, Mom had gained enough weight to be allowed outside the hospital, and the doctors encouraged Dad to visit at least once a month. Our time with him, already limited, was diminished even further.

During Dad's absences, Helen folded my brothers and I into the routines of her life. In many ways we became like her children, with Helen including us in one of her favorite activities—baseball games at Candlestick Park. She always bought tickets in the bleachers behind the left field fence. Together, we sat huddled under sleeping bags to keep warm from the damp fog sweeping in from the Bay. Even though I didn't understand what was happening on the field, I got a kick out of hearing Helen cheer for her favorite player, Willie Mays, the "Say Hey Kid." The suspense for me was not if the Giants might win the game, but whether I might cajole Helen into buying me a souvenir.

On Saturday afternoons, she brought us to horror movies on Mission Street, an area of town that was littered with trash—discarded hamburger cartons and empty packs of cigarettes—and people, many of whom appeared to have nothing better to do than stand around or sit on the sidewalk. It was a world away from our little house on Locust Street.

In the darkened theatre, I clutched her hand while Dracula, or some kind of nuclear-mutated monster—the Blob or Godzilla—wreaked havoc on its victims. This was a time before movie ratings, because nobody stopped Helen from dragging me in to witness such things. It was a miracle I was able to sleep at night. Perhaps it was because I knew that those movies were pretend and that Helen, sitting at my side, was real.

Just because Helen melded my brothers and I into her life didn't mean she was easy on us. She encased her love within a brittle shell and did not hesitate to threaten a whopping if we got even the slightest bit unruly. We knew that she threatened ten whoppings for every one she gave, but the thought of her thick hand paddling our rear ends was enough to cause obedience. As the youngest, I had it the easiest. Whenever Helen's friends visited the house, she always introduced me in the same way: "This here is Daniel," she would say, beaming. "He's my baby."

~

In December 1966, when I was four, Dad took Jimmy, John, and me to the Grossinger Resort in New York's Catskill Mountains for the celebration of his parents' 50th wedding anniversary. Practically the whole family was there, along with many friends. Only Mom was missing.

At the anniversary dinner, I watched one person after another rise from their chairs, stroll to the front of the room, and speak into a long, thin machine that sent their voices echoing throughout the room. I noticed how, when they spoke, the other diners ceased their conversations and turned to listen. Suddenly, I was out of my chair and striding to the front of the room. I had no idea what I wanted to say, only that I wanted the audience's attention.

I paused for a moment, gazing at the circle of smiling, expectant faces. And then I began to talk, marveling at the amplified sound of my own voice. Even though my words are lost to history, the laughter and applause wrapped me in a warm embrace. No matter what I said, the laughter increased, as if I was fiddling with the volume on Dad's stereo. I felt like one of the magicians I'd seen on television, pulling a string of multicolored handkerchiefs out of thin air.

Despite the evident popularity of my toast, Dad soon appeared at my side easing the microphone away. "I think that's enough," he whispered.

From that moment on, I desperately wanted to entertain people. Nothing felt as satisfying as standing in front of a crowd and lapping up their laughter. The laughter and approval were like a drug that I used more and more as time went on to stave off my unhappiness.

~

Mom's absence stretched on through my fifth birthday. Then, one day in early 1967, Dad announced that he was bringing all of us, Helen included, to visit Mom in Topeka.

I wonder what we looked like to other passengers at the Kansas City airport. My brothers and I wore coats and ties, and Helen wore a pillbox hat and black dress, as if on her way to church. While Dad and Jimmy waited to collect the luggage, Helen corralled John and me in the corner and muttered out of the side of her mouth that we better behave or else. I picture people smiling at us, thinking "what a dear family," wondering perhaps about Helen's role. How might they have reacted if they had leaned down to ask where our mother was and John or I had replied, "In Topeka, in a mental hospital."

Jimmy, being the oldest, remembers that the drive from the airport was tense. Several times Dad threatened to pull the car to the side of the road if we didn't behave. I can imagine the three of us crammed in the back, arguing over who touched whom and how one of us was encroaching on the other's space. Helen would have whirled around and said, "You boys better shush or there's gonna be trouble."

That night, we stayed at a two-story Holiday Inn, my first visit to a motel. Instead of anticipating the visit to Menninger, I immersed myself in distractions: the green paper ribbon that turned the toilet into a giant present, the plastic "do not disturb" signs, the ice machines. My excitement was tempered only by learning that John and Jimmy shared their own room, while I had to stay with Helen.

The next day, on the way to visit Mom, I threw my all-time greatest fit. Dad remembers I began to scream and cry uncontrollably, tossing myself on the lawn outside the Menninger campus. Because I have no memory of my emotions on that day, I sometimes look at five-year-olds and imagine how they might feel to have their Mom—the center of their world, their universe—disappear one day and not return.

I picture a little face contorted by grief. I hear the choking sobs and the hiccuping refrain: "I want my Mommy." Then I see the parent rocking the child back and forth, murmuring "Shhh, it's okay." In this case, Dad hoisted me over his shoulder like a bag of potatoes and carried me to the meeting.

Mom had gained weight by this time, but I don't remember if she looked unfamiliar, or what feelings I had upon seeing her for the first time in almost two years. Jimmy remembers that she appeared happy. That must have been a relief, though it might also have raised the question: How she could be happy so far away from home?

She showed us her new life. The greenhouse, where she tended rosemary, dill, and oregano was one of her favorite places. She explained that the herbs were used to make salad dressing for the hospital kitchen. We were introduced to her many friends, including Dr. Jacobs whom I must have liked. I still have a note that I wrote on the plane ride home asking Mom to let him know my arm was still attached to my body, a reference to some forgotten joke.

Menninger policy forbade patients' families from visiting their rooms. This was a particularly cruel blow—I was desperate to see where she lived, to sit on her bed and play with her jewelry, to picture her desk where she wrote us letters. These letters and a few phone calls were the most tangible proof of her continued existence. Instead, I stayed in the hotel each night while she and Dad spent time together. This only reinforced my imagination of Mom as a fairy princess, always just out of reach.

The visit ended and we said goodbye and returned to our lives in San Francisco without Mom. We must have asked when she was coming home, to which she would have replied truthfully, "I don't know." While my brothers and I would have left it at that, Dad must have responded with " but we need you." Dad was beginning to wonder whether Mom was ever going to come home. Dr. Jacobs worried about the same thing.

I wrote a note to Mom on the plane ride home, which I discovered many years later in one of her drawers.

Get Well (Please)

Right now I am on the plane. Even though I just left you a couple of hours ago, I miss you terribly. As I came home from Menninger I realized that I'm going to miss you a lot more, since now I've seen you and been with you.

Love, Daniel

~

Before she left for Menninger, Mom and Dad had agreed that the family required a bigger house. Dad also wanted to spare Mom the stress of having to move when she returned home. So, one day, he announced that we would be moving into a new house around the corner from 135 Locust Street. But this wasn't just any house—it was a Castle.

An investment my grandfather made years earlier on Dad's behalf had resulted in a great deal of money. The original $10,000 was now worth more than $1,000,000 (in 1967 dollars), allowing Dad to purchase the new house. Yet, when Dad tells me, as he sometimes does, that money doesn't buy happiness, he can point to this specific example. On his way back from picking up the check, he stopped to see Mom at Menninger. Years later, Dad explains that he would have happily returned all the money in exchange for Mom's health.

Our new house with its turrets and leaded windows sat like a fortress on the corner of Washington and Spruce streets, command-ing a view of the two red towers of the Golden Gate Bridge. The man who built the house had been one of the Bridge's engineers, and he had allowed his mind free rein on the design. Though only three stories, the house contained six bedrooms, six bathrooms, a library, living and dining rooms, a basement with a stage, and most unusual of all, an elevator. Best of all, if you knew just where to push on the paneled wood that lined the main hallway, secret doors opened revealing a bathroom, bar, and hidden passageway to the basement.

Dad must have smiled when he saw us running around the house, yelling "cool" at each new discovery. He must have felt proud, fulfilling the traditional male role. His wife would come home to the house of her dreams.

Or of her nightmares. When Mom first heard about the house, she anxiously asked Dr. Jacobs, "Who's going to keep it up?" Dad assured her she would get her all the help she needed. "And if you don't love it," he promised, "we can always move somewhere else."

But Mom was in no hurry to join us in the Castle. By mid-1967, she had not only recovered the weight she had lost before getting sick, her body kept right on gaining weight. Incredibly, the woman who left home at 74 pounds now weighed in at over 200 pounds. These days, treatment facilities would not allow such an extreme weight gain to occur, but in the 1960s there was little experience with anorexia nervosa treatment. Dr. Jacobs told Dad that both gaining weight and being underweight were two sides of the same coin—issues of control.

In 1967, the American Psychiatric Association had not yet created a diagnosis for anorexia nervosa. According to the definition later produced, Mom no longer met the diagnosis. Yet her departure from Menninger became a difficult issue. While the stay had saved her life, Dr. Jacobs believed she would have needed as long as four to five years to get better. As he later told me, "Of course she had other obligations that couldn't be neglected. If we'd kept her and she got better but had no family to go back to, that would have been a disaster." He told her there was nothing more Menninger could do and that it was time to return to her family.

Mom was reluctant to leave as well. She had many friends at Menninger, and she was never stigmatized there for being underweight or overweight. Her warm relationship with Dr. Jacobs, who was never too busy to listen to her deepest thoughts and concerns, was something she couldn't replicate with her husband. She didn't have to be a wife, or mother, or take care of a big house, or manage a busy and pressured social calendar. "Of course she was happy there," Dad later said. "She had no responsibilities."

Dr. Jacobs told me that some patients never left Topeka, deciding to remain there either with their families moving close by or not. I sometimes wonder what might have happened if Mom had just decided to stay. Would Dad have agreed to move us all to Kansas? Would she have even wanted that? How much differently would all of our lives have turned out?

At Lake Tahoe, just before she began to exhibit the first signs of anorexia nervosa, Mom had felt let down by the men in her life— her father and husband—who would not defend her from Isabel. As the time came to leave Menninger, did she once again feel betrayed—this time by Dad and Dr. Jacobs—who insisted it was time for her to go? Did this reinforce for her a feeling of lacking control over her life?

Many years later, when I tried to contact Dr. Jacobs to discuss his memories of Mom, he wouldn't answer my letters. He only agreed to meet after I informed him I was coming to Topeka anyway. When he sat across from me in a deserted hotel lobby and removed his hat and scarf, I was immediately taken by his blue eyes, the hint of North Carolina drawl in his voice, and his obvious compassion. After we exchanged pleasantries, he addressed his lack of response to my inquiries.

"I really didn't want to have this meeting," he said.

"Because of confidentiality issues?" I asked, aware that this might be a concern for a psychiatrist.

"No," he said, "that wasn't it at all. It was because it ended so badly. I will never forget the anger in your mother's eyes when your father came to take her back to San Francisco."

"She didn't want to go?" I asked.

"She didn't want to go," he replied.

At the age of five, I could not have understood how Mom might feel ambivalent about rejoining her family. But I have since accepted the possibility that she could have both loved and missed us, and at the same time, yearned to be free. As Tobias Woolf has described his own mother's conflicting desires in *This Boy's Life*, "the human heart is a dark forest."

Mom and Dad spared us from any direct knowledge of her ambivalence. Perhaps we sensed it at a deeper level; children are remarkably intuitive. As a grown man though, my awareness was buried deep. I could only stare with surprise at Dr. Jacobs, his words repeating in my mind, "She didn't want to go."

3

HOME

One evening, in mid-1967, Dad ushered us into the library for a family meeting. This room, with its large fireplace, overstuffed bookshelves and Dad's ebony Eames chair, was a haven for me. Other parts of the house, particularly the living and dining rooms, were off limits—just for show. The library, with its many scents—cigarettes, cigars, or my favorite, cherry pipe tobacco—was comfortable. It housed the family chess set with its solid wooden pieces that felt so satisfying to slide around the board. I liked to watch Dad playing John or Jimmy at chess, waiting for the day when I would sit across from him.

My brothers and I climbed onto the couch facing the fireplace, jostling each other for room. Dad stood in front of us, one arm resting on the mantel and the other cradling a pipe, as if he was a sergeant preparing to address his troops. He always looked pretty serious to me, so it was hard to guess whether the news would be good or bad.

"Boys, I have an announcement," he began. "Your mother will be coming home soon. I know you'll welcome her back appropriately. She is still very fragile, and this is going to be a difficult transition. It's important that you try your best not to upset her. Do you think you can do that? Can I count on you?"

At one time, holding a microphone in hand, I had discovered the ability to make people happy. Now Dad revealed the other side of the Faustian bargain: I also had the power to injure, to make Mom sick. His words sent a chill through the three of us. If unconsciously, we already felt responsible for Mom's illness and departure, we now knew explicitly that we had some responsibility for her continued health.

Looking back, I feel sorry for us boys sitting quietly in that cozy, book-stuffed library. For this moment represents the end of our innocence. We now knew that if we continued to act like children, to cry or express anger or tell our parents that we hated them, this might drive Mom thousands of miles away. Perhaps next time she might not return.

My brothers and I simply nodded our heads, eager to please.

"Yes, of course, you can count on us, Dad."

~

I can picture Mom riding home from the airport in Dad's Ford Thunderbird, but I cannot imagine how she was feeling. Was she excited to return to her husband and children? She certainly carried anxiety about the new house. She must also have felt ambivalent about her new body size—over 200 pounds—given that her initial diet goal, which began the whole cascading disaster, was to get to 130 pounds. In Topeka, she had apparently been at peace with her weight. In San Francisco, where she would attend the opera, symphony, and ballet with old friends, she may have thought it a different story.

I see the car cresting the Spruce Street hill and Mom glimpsing the Castle for the first time. Did she see it as a Tudor palace, her own Hampton Court? (Years later, she would set her alarm for 2 A.M. so as not to miss Prince Charles and Princess Diana's wedding.) Or did the turrets and metallic brown garage doors remind her of some sort of medieval dungeon?

And how did we react, her three sons, when she walked in the door with a different body? Despite Dad's warnings, did one of us ask her how she had gotten so fat? It is possible. Or maybe we smothered her in hugs and kisses and made her feel welcome and loved in her new surroundings. I hope so.

By this time I was attending Marin Country Day School with my two brothers, across the Golden Gate Bridge from San Francisco. Each afternoon the school bus dropped us at the corner outside the house, and we rushed up the back stairs and into the kitchen, the nerve center of the Castle. "Hi Mom, Hi Helen," we'd yell and head immediately for the two white cabinet doors behind which hid the snacks—pretzels and cookies and whatever happened to be in vogue at the moment, like Space Sticks, "the breakfast of astronauts."

Jimmy and John would gather their stash and quickly disappear, either up to their rooms or down to Julius Kahn playground to play basketball or tennis. I usually stayed in the kitchen, to bask in the attention of the two most important people in my life, Mom and Helen.

Often the same scene was repeated. I would gather my pretzels and cookies and a glass of milk and sit down at the kitchen table. Helen would be standing at the stove, stirring the turkey gravy, brown and sizzling. Mom would stand at the butcher block table, leafing through copies of *Gourmet*. Swinging my feet under the table, I would observe that Mom and Helen pursued their separate activities as if some hidden charge flowed between them.

Then something would spark. Perhaps Mom would go over to poke the turkey with a fork.

"Do you think it's fully done, Helen?" she would ask, one eye squinched down with skepticism.

"Mrs. Becker," Helen would reply, always drawing her name with a long Southern dialect, "I been fixing turkeys for 20 years. I should rightly know when it's done."

"There's no need to snap at me," Mom would say. "I was just asking the question."

Then Helen would mutter under her breath, and as if on a static-filled radio, out would come the word—"shit."

Mom's fork rattled to the floor. "What did you say?"

"Nothing Mrs. Becker, I didn't say nothing."

"I want to know what you said. It was something about me."

"I didn't say nothing. I'm just going about my business."

"This is my house, Helen. You have to treat me with respect in my own house."

And then the silence descended again, and the two of them went back to working furiously on their separate activities. I gathered up my snacks and shuffled towards the door, my eyes focused on the floor. If things were really bad, neither of them noticed. But if they were only half bad Mom would look up and ask, "Where you going Daniel Boone?"

"Just up to my room," I'd say, "to look at my baseball cards." Later on, sorting the cards on my blue carpet, I might hear hollering coming from the kitchen. I couldn't make out the words and that suited me fine.

~

Mom threw herself into two projects: decorating the Castle and losing the extra pounds she had gained in Topeka. Shedding so much weight would be a daunting task to most people, but Mom had already proven herself a remarkably good dieter. John remembers her telling someone proudly on the phone, perhaps six months later, that she had lost 60 pounds, which would have put her in the range of 140 pounds. They were pounds she would never regain.

I find it almost impossible to believe she ever weighed this much. But then I look back at photographs and see her filled-out face and full body, so different from the gaunt woman in my memories. There I am in the pictures and there is Dad and my brothers. So it must be true, no matter how much my mind rejects the possibility.

Collaborating with her close friend Jerry, an interior decorator, Mom set about transforming the Castle. Many of the items that turned up at this time struck me as just plain odd. For the family room, Jerry convinced Mom to hang a frameless oil painting of an oversized rooster in a barn. There was also a *papier-mâché* cow's head that gazed down from one of the kitchen's walls, and another painting of a gigantic yellow dog lying in a canyon while a tiny plane flies overhead. It looked like a drawing you might find tucked in the pages of *The Little Prince*. Visitors sometimes asked me if I had made the drawing.

"Oh no," I would reply. "It's by someone famous."

~

It was about this time in 1970 when I was eight, John was ten, and Jimmy was thirteen that Jimmy began to shut his bedroom door and spend hours listening to rock music on his stereo headphones. He took to wearing them after Dad asked him one too many times to "turn down that awful music." Jimmy forbade Helen from cleaning his room, which had grown into an accumulation of books, clothes, record jackets, candles, and other objects dotting the black carpet. Helen never reconciled herself to the mess in Jimmy's room, and she grumbled about it constantly, like an itch she was forbidden to scratch.

His bedroom was at the top of the stairs on the second floor. Often, as I walked past, I felt a draft blowing from under his door. I wondered why he kept his windows wide open even when, as was often the case in our neighborhood, the weather was cold and foggy.

The changes in Jimmy seemed to reflect a larger tumult, the extent of which I could not fully grasp. I noticed that someone had written "the war" in white paint at the bottom of all the neighborhood stop signs. Mom no longer kept grapes in a bowl on the kitchen table because Jimmy had forbidden her to do so. She said it had something to do with a man named Cesar Chavez and his support of farm workers. Sometimes when we acted up, Helen would threaten to leave John and me "down on Haight Street with the hippies."

It grew harder to get through a whole dinner without Dad and Jimmy having an argument. Dad might ask Jimmy to clean up his room and Jimmy would say something about invasion of privacy and Dad might say this was his house and all of a sudden Jimmy was bolting from the table and stomping up the stairs to his room. Sometimes, he refused to come down for dinner at all. I noticed the rest of us ate in a kind of heightened silence, pretending that his absence didn't matter, even as it pressed down on us.

In those days, I never thought much about Mom and Dad's relationship. It seemed normal, even romantic. Each Friday, Dad brought home a bouquet of flowers from the street vendor outside his downtown office. Each night, as soon as he arrived home, Mom would fix him a Scotch and water and the two of them would huddle at the kitchen table, recounting their days. Mom later told us that she was Dad's source of intelligence, sharing with him gossip and bits of news she had picked up from her friends. In return, Dad told her about what was happening in the business and any pressures he might be under at work.

Sometimes, as children do, we would ask Mom and Dad to repeat the story of how they met. Dad had been in the hospital with a broken ankle from a skiing accident, and Mom called him on the advice of a mutual friend. They became engaged after only five weeks. When Dad was ready to propose, he couldn't get down on his knee because he was still in a cast.

Dad, at 27, still lived at home with his parents. "Sometimes I think your father married me just to get out of the house," Mom would say with a laugh. But there's no doubt they had been in love. Years later, I discovered a letter Mom had sent to her parents from her honeymoon in Jamaica. "Each day is better than the last," she wrote. "I discover more wonderful qualities about Alan every day." As Dad recalls: "It was the perfect marriage. We were both Jewish, we had many friends in common, our families liked each other, we had similar educations and dreams for the future."

Whatever difficulties they had were kept private. Sometimes we heard Mom sputter when Dad was again late for dinner or invited someone over at the last minute without letting Mom know. But these seemed like minor complaints, typical of all husbands and wives.

The conflicts with Jimmy, in contrast, were immediate and dramatic—yelling, slamming doors, worried parental huddles. They crowded out more difficult topics, like whether Mom had completely recovered from her illness, or what role, if any, her relationship with Dad or the rest of us played into it, or perhaps most important, what might need to change in the family for her to stay healthy.

~

Thanks to Dad's new wealth, we traveled to Europe, sailing on the *S.S. France* from New York to Southampton, England. Jimmy had gone ahead and was to meet us in Europe, so it was only Mom, Dad, John, and I on the ship. One night, in a pique of showing off, I announced that I was prepared to eat snails. John eyed me with a combination of horror and disgust. Mom and Dad beamed with pride. They summoned the waiter over and ordered "a plate of escargot for the young man."

I had not yet understood that Mom's constant discussion about food and her obsession with particular restaurants might be un-healthy. On this trip I cannot recall any of the unpleasant scenes that eventually came to dominate our restaurant experiences with her. Maybe Mom was healthy at this point, or maybe I have simply forgotten. I sought to please her by sampling all kinds of foods, including the snails.

My pride lasted exactly the length of time it took for the six curled shells to be set down with a flourish in front of me. Dad demonstrated how to use the fork to extract the snail's meat from the shell. I could feel the eyes upon me as I examined the slimy, yellowish-green piece of rubber. I thrust it in my mouth, chewed a couple of times, swallowed, and almost choked with disgust. Dad finished the rest while Mom flashed a triumphant grin.

Later that night, Dad offered John and me a dollar each if we would ask Mom to dance. The ship had a main ballroom where couples could twirl away the evenings. Being adolescents, we were too shy to take him up on the offer. Later, after hustling us off to bed, they won a trophy in the dance contest.

This picture of Mom and Dad, sweeping across the floor amidst the other couples, is an image I keep locked in a little treasure box in my mind. I do not open this box often, buried as it is beneath layers of sadness. But occasionally I recall one of these mental pictures and bring it up to the light, examining it from every angle until storing it for the next time.

Mom adored England and I quickly copied her enthusiasm. She liked to recall her first visit there as a junior in college. This was soon after World War II when she'd witnessed damage from the war, something that had fueled her curiosity for history. Upon our arrival in London she bought me a booklet listing all of the kings and queens of England from William the Conqueror on down. I set about memorizing them.

"History is cool," I told Mom and Dad after our day at the Tower of London where we had tiptoed through the torture chambers, and I had imagined leather-hooded guards cackling at their prisoners.

In Italy we stayed at the Villa d'Este, a fashionable resort where we saw Dad fold a wad of bills in his palm and transfer it to the bellhop with a handshake. We spent the rest of the trip practicing this trick, certain that we would spend the rest of our lives visiting places like this.

One day, left to myself, I went off to explore, followed a little stream, and wound up far from the hotel grounds. Fighting down panic, I walked into a barbershop and asked if anyone knew how to get to the Villa d'Este. The barbers shrugged their shoulders with a lack of comprehension, until I pulled out a box of matches with the hotel's insignia emblazoned across the top. This set off a round of incomprehensible conversation that ended with me being hustled into a taxi and winding up back at the hotel's main entrance.

~

When we arrived in Paris, Dad and I decided we wanted to eat Chinese food and hopped into a cab.

"Do you speak English?" Dad asked the driver.

"Yes, *monsieur*."

"Take us to the best Chinese restaurant in Paris."

"*Monsieur*, if it is good Chinese food you want, I suggest you go to San Francisco."

I squealed with delight.

But in Paris, things changed for the worse. Dad had to fly home, as his business had suffered a blow. He left immediately to deal with the fallout, something concerning President Nixon devaluing the dollar. The night he departed, my brothers and I wound up in a screaming fight with Mom, which was bred out of fear on both sides. For the first time since her return from Menninger, Mom was solely responsible for the three of us, and we were in a foreign country where she didn't speak the language. For our part, we may have feared no longer having Dad as a buffer. Now we were solely responsible for Mom and her health.

While we were crying and screaming at one another, did Mom think back to the manicured lawns and comfortable wooden benches at Menninger where she sat and talked with Dr. Jacobs? Or did she think about her days before us, the summers at horse camp and her undergraduate years? Or her wedding to Dad at the Waldorf-Astoria Hotel? Or the decision to move to San Francisco and the illness that seemed to come out of nowhere?

I did not help to relieve her anxieties. The morning we were to leave Paris for Copenhagen, I wandered off to buy a postcard at the corner store and wound up hopelessly lost yet again. Knowing I was late, I recalled my Italy experience and hailed a cab. "Ritz Hotel," I told the cabbie in my best French accent. As the taxi pulled up to the curb, there stood Mom, Jimmy, and John fronted by an impressive pile of luggage. I hopped out, strode confidently up to Mom and, before she could say anything, told her I needed five francs to pay the cabdriver. She was so taken aback she forgot to scold me and simply reached for the coins.

We made it through the rest of the trip without fighting. Mom began to demonstrate the role that she would increasingly come to play in the future, less like a Mom and more like a friend. In Copenhagen she noticed my excitement at the lack of a drinking age and allowed me to taste my first beer. She took us to the Danish baths where the hot pools were followed by dips in an ice-cold plunge, and we spent the afternoon lazing on deck chairs. We visited Hamlet's Castle (bigger than our own) and the famous Mermaid sculpture in Copenhagen harbor, a tribute to Hans Christian Anderson. On the 14-hour flight home, we received pilot wings and the flight attendant invited us to visit the cockpit and talk to the captain.

~

Back in San Francisco, Mom continued to delight in my willing-ness to try new foods. I delighted in her delight, developing a passion for artichokes. Mom showed me how to dip the leaves in butter and how to find the heart. She cut out a large picture of an artichoke from a magazine, and it gained the most prominent position on my bedroom bulletin board.

Helen also took pleasure in my increased interest in food. Only now do I see that the two of them might have used food to com-pete for my attention. Both spent most days in the kitchen battling constantly about cooking. Food was the soft spot in each of their hearts.

Family dinners continued to be interrupted by screaming matches between Jimmy and Dad. Occasionally, I noticed that Mom talked a lot during dinner, and it took her a long time to finish her meal. I also noticed that sometimes she would bring her fork up to her mouth two, three, or even four times before finally taking a bite. I never thought much of it at the time. Only now, looking back, do I see her illness was continuing to fester.

4

NUMB

In the five years since Mom's homecoming, I had come to know her voice and laughter and the way the corners of her eyes crinkled when she found something I said amusing. I knew each afternoon when I came home from school, she would be in the kitchen waiting to greet me and ask me about my day. I knew I was special to her, her very own "Daniel Boone." Then, she was gone, departing for Menninger again in the spring of 1972.

Obviously, there were things I didn't know. That she had once again been exhibiting the signs of anorexia nervosa, for example.

That she hadn't really been eating. That her weight had been steadily dropping. Had I been aware of some of the telltale behaviors, perhaps I might have had an idea that something wasn't quite right.

Looking back, I sometimes wonder how I didn't notice. I have talked about it with Jimmy and John. Their experience was the same—the announcement of Mom's impending departure hit them in the same way, like a sucker punch when we didn't know we were in the ring. Perhaps I would have braced myself for the oncoming blow had I known that something was wrong. But the more I have learned about anorexia nervosa, the more I have come to understand that hiding is what anorexics do. It's their peculiar expertise. Mom focused her considerable intellect on finding ways to mask her lack of eating.

We were reassured by Dad that Mom's return to Menninger was a positive step, a way to stave off further illness, although it was hard for me to judge. I still had no idea what was wrong with her—and Dad never sat us down to explain. Even in the early 1970s, anorexia nervosa remained a rare and relatively unstudied illness. During one of his visits to Menninger, Dad asked the social worker assigned to Mom's case for something to read about anorexia, but was told, "Don't bother, you won't understand it anyway."

In reality, there were no books on eating disorders yet, though Dad could have dug up the writings of Dr. Richard Morton, an English physician who, in 1689, provided the first description of an anorexia nervosa patient in medical literature. He detailed an 18-year-old girl who had stopped having her period, explaining his reasoning as due to "a multitude of cares and passions of the mind":

> I do not remember that I did ever in all my practice
> see one, that was conversant with the living so much
> wasted with the greatest degree of a consumption (like a

skeleton only clad with skin), yet there was no fever, but on the contrary a coldness of the whole body; no cough, or difficulty of breathing, nor an appearance of any other distemper of the lungs or of any other entrails. Only her appetite was diminished and her digestion uneasy, with fainting fits which did frequently return upon her.[2]

His patient died three months later during a fainting fit.

Dad might also have reviewed the works of Charles Lesegue, a French neurologist, and Sir William Gull, another British doctor, both of whom are credited with discovering and naming the illness in the late 1800s. Or the case studies of Hilde Bruch, a pioneer in the field of eating disorders who began to write about the disease in the 1950s. But even had Dad waded through this dense literature, riddled with terms like etiology, psychosomatic symptoms, and menarche, an explanation for the cause of anorexia nervosa would have remained maddeningly out of reach.

Only in 1978, several years after Mom had completed her second stay at Menninger, did Hilde Bruch publish *The Golden Cage*, the first book on anorexia nervosa written for the public. That same year, ABC Television broadcast a Hallmark Hall of Fame movie based on Steven Levenkron's novel, *The Best Little Girl in the World*, which depicted the tribulations faced by the 15-year-old character, Kessa Dietrich. In the first scene, Kessa is told by her ballet instructor to lose weight in order to improve as a dancer. The story goes downhill from there. The portrait of anorexia nervosa that emerged from this increased attention—an illness that primarily struck adolescent girls—had little to do with Mom, however, who was 42 when she departed for Menninger the second time.

I have often wondered why I never sought to read anything about anorexia nervosa until after Mom's death. Maybe it was because nobody ever gave us a clear explanation. Or maybe it was because we learned early on that to ask Mom about it might cause the mysterious illness to return. All I knew was that she was somehow sicker and had to go away to get better. Unbeknownst to me, other family members had developed their own theories. When Mom first went to Menninger, her father, Irving, proposed an outlandish idea to Dad: "Maybe she fell off a horse during one of her summers at camp. Maybe she hit her head and we never knew about it."

~

I was ten years old, a third grader at a private school in Marin County during Mom's second departure. The school was a haven. It gave me a platform for showing off—and, as I realized later, escaping. There was the time my teacher told me to remove the gum from my mouth and, instead of throwing it the garbage, I stuck it behind my ear where it became entangled in my hair. The teacher had to cut it out, much to the class's amusement and my delight at being center stage. Because both of my brothers also went there, and Dad served on the Board of Trustees, everyone knew who I was.

Although my behavior hadn't changed much since Mom's second departure, something was going on inside of me. Some of the theories of John Bowlby, a British psychologist, provide insight into what might have been happening. Bowlby studied the impact caused by separation of young children from their mothers, and he is credited with coining the term *attachment theory*. He points to three stages in a young child's reaction to a mother's absence. The initial phase is protest, where the distressed child cries and rejects potential substitutes. The second phase is despair, where the crying and protests are replaced by deep mourning. Because the child tends to be quiet in this stage, it can often be misinterpreted as a lessening of anxiety.

Detachment is the third stage, where the child resumes interest in his or her surroundings and may even appear sociable and happy. As Bowlby puts it, "To some, this change seems satisfactory," but he also identifies long-term consequences. The child "will appear cheerful and adapted to his unusual situation and apparently easy and unafraid of anyone. But this sociability is superficial: he no longer appears to care for anyone."

Bowlby's theories might explain how certain seeds, that would not flower for many years, were planted. In the meantime, nobody noticed much of a change in my demeanor.

The changes were more apparent in my brothers. John and I had always played together, if somewhat uneasily, creating sports leagues out of tabletop electronic football and hockey games. We drafted teams, named the inanimate pieces after real players, and kept statistics in spiral-ringed notebooks. John had always harbored a temper, and after Mom's leaving we never seemed to finish a game without it devolving into a fight. I learned to read John like a geologist studying a volcano, noting the magma's movement toward the surface and relying on quickness to escape at the first sign of eruption. When he began to blow, I would dash downstairs to the guest bathroom that could be locked from the inside, a safe place to wait him out.

After a particularly narrow escape, I heard a thumping sound and turned to watch the bathroom door bow inwards. As I cowered toward the toilet, John's sneaker splintered the wood and wiggled around like it was seeking me out. John and I had reached a new threshold of potential violence. Luckily, Helen arrived just at this moment, threatening us both with whoppings.

Jimmy grew more sullen and withdrawn. His relationship with Dad mirrored the distrust and threats then being lobbed between the United States and Soviet Union. Mom's absence had robbed Jimmy of his great ally, and his anger was pointed toward a central target—Dad. "I felt betrayed," he later explained. "I was mad at her for leaving me alone with Dad like that."

I have since thought a lot about Jimmy's experience. Five years older than I, three years older than John, he was touched by Mom's departures most acutely. One event that created shock waves was Jimmy's expulsion from Marin Country Day School near his eighth grade graduation. He had been caught smoking marijuana behind a campus building and was thrown out of school along with a couple of other boys from our neighborhood. In retrospect, the event was fraught with symbolism. Dad was a respected member of the school establishment, and Jimmy was about to move on to high school. If there was ever a good time to blow things up in protest, this was it.

I became an instant celebrity among my friends. For the first time, I realized the value of having a brother who was a rebel and a hippie. That coolness could be passed along by association, at least in others' eyes. Being Jimmy Becker's brother added to my already considerable cachet at the school.

While the Castle seethed with bitterness, Jimmy and John were sent to their own psychiatrists. Jimmy was assigned to a prominent woman who had studied under Bruno Bettelheim and kept an office in the then-sleepy hamlet of Mill Valley. On Friday afternoons, instead of riding the school bus home, Helen drove us to Mill Valley for Jimmy's appointment. After he disappeared into the psychiatrist's office, Helen took John and me to the Book Depot, a former railroad station converted to a bookstore and café.

While John and I lay on the floor reading *Archie* and *Richie Rich* comic books, Helen rested at a wooden table, chewing on a toothpick and leafing through advertisements in the newspaper. When we grew restless, Helen bought us hot chocolate and took us outside, where she smoked a Pall Mall and we gazed up at the towering redwood trees that reminded me of *Jack and the Beanstalk*.

Later, I watched Jimmy in the front seat and longed to know what had transpired in that office. Everything was so maddeningly secret in those days, and Jimmy was already so removed from John and me—older, wiser, cooler. He disdained us for our youth and our neutral position with Dad. His mysterious relationship with the psychiatrist only put him further out of reach.

John was sent to visit Dr. Arthur Armstrong, whose office, only a block from the Castle, was across the street from Colonial Liquor where all the neighborhood kids spent their allowances on candy. In contrast to Jimmy's mysterious visits, it was no secret what took place during John's sessions.

"What did you and Dr. Armstrong talk about today?" Dad asked at dinner each Thursday, the evening of John's weekly appointment.

"We played chess," John would unfailingly reply.

John refused to speak to Dr. Armstrong, so the two of them spent their sessions engaged in a silent game of chess. When the allotted time expired, John headed home, perhaps stopping at Colonial to purchase a pink bubble gum cigar or a pack of Twinkies. One Thursday evening, as if it was an afterthought, Dad announced that John would no longer be meeting with Dr. Armstrong.

At Christmas, before that happened, I noticed how each of Jimmy and John's psychiatrists had given them a present. "I want a psychiatrist too," I said to Mom on the phone, but my turn would have to wait.

Instead, Dad drove me to the small town of Benicia to examine a desk he thought might fit well in my room. When we entered the antique shop and he pointed to the piece he had in mind, I had to stifle an impulse to raise my arms in elation. It was crafted from wood the color of maple syrup and consisted of two stands of drawers and a main section that lay across the top. The drawer handles were brass and resembled upside down teacups sliced in half. I pictured the jealous looks on my brothers' faces after the desk would be assembled in my room.

"Do you like it?" Dad asked.

"I guess it will work," I said, trying to sound mature.

My writing habit began prior to Mom returning to Menninger. I had discovered, with my first story, an account of the daily lives of the oblong green residents of Pickleville, that writing was another way to entertain people. But unlike writers who allow their work to marinate, I needed immediate gratification. I'd sought Mom out in the kitchen as soon as I penned the last line of *Pickleville*, handing her the four-page manuscript. It's "hot off the press" I had exclaimed, watching for her response. When she proclaimed it "wonderful, marvelous, a great effort," I immediately printed her review on the front cover.

Writing was my way of reassuring Mom that I was thinking about her, loved her, and hoped she would come home as soon as possible. I was particularly taken with poetry, though I had yet to realize that poems could be written in anything other than rhymes. I spent hours poring over the dictionary, searching for words that sounded alike. I hoped to entertain Mom and keep her from getting too sad and lonely.

I wrote a poem to her during this time, which provides a window to my mindset:

Mom,

Even though you're not with us
I know you're getting well

But when you will be back with us
No one can really tell.
I hope that it will be soon though
Because I really miss you
And when you're not around me
My life is a big to-do.
You know that I love you very much
So could you please do a favor for me?
Can you please get better just as quick as you can?
And then get home just as quick as can be.

–Daniel, age 10

~

After Mom had been away for another six months, she came home for a visit. Her first couple of days back I watched her like a CIA agent trying to detect a secret code. Nothing stuck out—if there was something different about her from when she left, I didn't see it. This seemed to confirm the futility of trying to understand what was wrong. She appeared happy: talking, smiling, saying how much she missed us. I soon gave up trying to figure anything out and blossomed in the sunshine of her presence. When I wasn't with her, I worked at my desk to ensure she had a large stack of new poems to bring back to Menninger.

One afternoon, while she was in her dressing room looking through clothes, I asked if I could skip Sunday school that week to spend more time with her. My motives were not entirely pure. I loathed Sunday school and did anything to avoid it, even if it meant playing on Mom's heartstrings.

"I'm sorry dear," she said, "but your father insists you go."

Sensing hesitation in her voice, I decided to take an offensive approach.

"You're mean," I said, dipping into my grab bag of verbal weapons. "I guess you don't care about my feelings."

"Now honey, you know that I care about your feelings."

For some reason, this made me even angrier.

"You don't care about us at all. If you did, you wouldn't go away so much."

In the ensuing silence, my remark hung in the air like an arrow in slow motion creeping toward its mark. After what seemed a great deal of time, Mom emerged from the dressing room carrying her suitcase and threw it open on the bed.

"If I'm not going to be appreciated in my house, I might as well go back to Menninger right now." She disappeared back into the dressing room and emerged a moment later clutching an armful of clothes that were dumped into the suitcase. Then she put her hand over her eyes and began to cry.

I turned and ran from the room, heading instinctively for a small bedroom off the kitchen. The room had an attached bathroom with a shower that nobody used, and I climbed into it, closed the curtain, and hugged my knees close to my chest trying to stifle my sobs so I wouldn't be discovered. I had already learned that absence was a good way to hurt people you love.

I waited in the shower stall, occasionally peeking around the curtain at a little picnic basket of strawberry-shaped soaps that rested on top of the toilet. I had bought these soaps as a gift for Mom one Mother's Day years before. They remained in their cellophane wrapping. Eventually, I heard voices and could just make out Mom asking Helen if she had seen me. I strained to detect any anguish in Mom's voice, but was thwarted by the wall's muffling effect.

When I finally realized that nobody was going to discover me, I began to lose interest in the effort. The problem became how to reveal myself without diminishing the victory. I decided I would neither apologize nor forgive.

As soon as I stepped into the kitchen, Mom rushed over and gathered me in a tight embrace. After a few moments, she held me out at arm's length, much the way Dad did when reassuring us that Mom's departures had nothing to do with my brothers and me.

"I should never have said I was going to leave like that. I'm so sorry."

And my willpower dissolved into a puddle. "That's okay," I reassured her. "I know you didn't mean it."

A few days later, she left again.

~

When I wasn't writing poems and stories, I listened to music on my box-like record player. I had the LPs of *Camelot* and *My Fair Lady* and the 45s of "It's a Small World After All" and "The Yellow Rose of Texas," but I had started to hear rock and roll music on my bedside radio and wanted to learn more about it. One evening, I knocked on Jimmy's door (no one entered his room without permission) to ask about borrowing some of his records. His collection was a neighborhood legend, occupying several rows of bookshelves.

He cracked open the door and stared blankly as I stammered out my request. I saw my frightened expression reflected in his round, tinted glasses. But instead of the dismissal I expected, he ushered me into the room. As always, the windows were wide open and the curtains fluttered in the breeze. He motioned for me to sit in his Naugahyde reclining chair, then turned to the wall of albums, cocking his head to read the tiny writing on the spines. The way he extracted the album from the dust jacket resembled how a mother might handle an infant. Although clothes, books, and other junk were scattered everywhere, not one album lacked a dust jacket, and each record resided on the shelf in alphabetical order.

I grew restless, but stifled myself for fear of disturbing the mood and being pointed toward the door. Finally, Jimmy held out two albums, but first he provided elaborate details about the consequences should I return them in anything other than mint condition. I nodded gravely as he placed in my hands *Stand Up* by Jethro Tull, then the Grateful Dead's *American Beauty*.

I was drawn first to the Jethro Tull album because when I opened it, the band members popped up in three dimensions, as if it was a children's book. I also already knew the song "Bungle in the Jungle" from the radio. But then I listened to the first track on *American Beauty*, a song called "Ripple." A few weeks later, after Jimmy demanded the record's return, I purchased my own copy.

Something in the words found a harbor in my soul: *Ripple in still water, when there is no pebble tossed, no wind to blow.*

5

Appearances

In the summer of 1973, Mom floated back to the Castle as
if she'd never been gone. Unlike her previous return, Dad did
not take my brothers and I aside to issue any special instructions.
By then, we were old enough to know that our job was to make
Mom feel welcome and, under no circumstances, do anything to
upset her. This time Mom looked the same as when she had left.
Her visit home earlier in the year, plus the many hours I'd imagined
her face in front of me while I wrote stories and poems, added to

the impression that she had barely been gone. It was almost as if I came down to breakfast one morning to find Mom back from an extended vacation.

I hadn't realized until then how much I missed our connection. She always asked about my day, whether anything unusual had happened, and if I wanted to invite any friends over for dinner. She intuited if anything was the slightest bit amiss and could always coax it out, whether I intended to share it or not. Though Helen and Dad made me feel loved, I couldn't share my inner self with them. With Mom it was effortless.

Because we never discussed the illness at home, I assumed that she had been cured. I was 11 years old and I had no knowledge otherwise. Only Dad knew that the Menninger doctors had discharged her with an uncertain prognosis, believing there was nothing more they could do. Only Dad knew that she remained gripped by the fear of gaining weight and an unhealthy obsession with food.

~

Our household had grown somewhat chaotic without Mom, despite my illusion that she'd barely been gone. Jimmy and Dad had largely stopped speaking, which in my view was preferable to the explosions that otherwise occurred. It was as if they were biding time until Mom came home to smooth out the situation. She immediately sought to address one of Dad's primary irritants—the length of Jimmy's hair.

Dad had always been preoccupied with appearances. He came by it honestly; his own father never appeared in public without a fresh flower in his boutonniere. Dad's hair was always short, never in danger of brushing his ears, and he was never unshaven. Thanks to a polishing machine he kept in his dressing room, his shoes always gleamed, matching the cleanliness of his suit and tie combination. The smell of cologne trailed after him.

Given Dad's fastidiousness, I cannot understand how Jimmy avoided cutting his hair for over two years. "Your brother has the longest hair of anyone in the neighborhood," my friends exclaimed with admiration, when Jimmy was 16. "He's a real hippie."

Discipline was never one of Mom's strong points, so it was a miracle when she announced that Jimmy was going to a barbershop. "Thank God and the Lord have mercy," Helen said. I still have no idea how Mom convinced Jimmy to take this step. She seemed to have a special way with all of us.

Later, I overheard her describing the hair cutting experience to a friend on the phone. "That's right," she said, "the barber discovered a peach pit that had gotten buried in there. I ended up giving him a $20 tip!"

~

Dinner parties were held at our house almost every week, with larger affairs—fundraisers and receptions for political or cultural causes—about once a month. It seems ironic that someone like Mom, who couldn't nourish her own body, would choose to host these extravagant events. Not only did she insist on orchestrating every aspect of the parties, Mom often hired a battery of caterers as well. It wasn't clear where she had learned these skills. Her parents, Irving and Isabel, never invited anyone to their home, entertaining exclusively in restaurants.

Often, when I came home from school, the kitchen was invaded by these caterers. Mom's favorite was a Japanese woman named Yama, who was short, bespectacled, and friendly, though not warm. Unlike Helen, who loved to share samples of her cooking, Yama gave only small bites and we somehow knew not to ask for more. She always brought several helpers who would peel vegetables over the sink or keep watch over the various pots heating on the six-burner restaurant stove Mom had purchased.

The caterers' presence meant I could not linger over an afternoon snack and the *San Francisco Chronicle's* sports pages at the kitchen table. Instead, Helen allowed one quick visit to the snack cabinet to gather pretzels and corn chips before shooing me out the door, along with the hissing admonition to "keep your butt out of here." Worse, it meant that at some point in the evening, my brothers and I would be forced to make an appearance at the ensuing dinner party.

After the guests had arrived, and the smell of cigarette smoke and murmur of conversation had drifted up to our bedrooms, we each waited, with exquisite sensitivity, for Mom's or Dad's footsteps on the stairs. We knew it would soon be followed with the dreaded, "Boys, come down and say hello to the guests." Once in the living room, we drifted from person to person, pretending to smile and listen attentively while being told how much we had grown and how handsome we had become.

Appearances took over every aspect of our lives. At home, we never acknowledged Mom's perplexing illness. The words *anorexia nervosa* were never uttered by my parents or anyone else. Our presentation to the guests confirmed that we were a normal family, that all was well in our home. I was particularly receptive to this message. It is one of the main reasons I never dwelled on our unusual circumstances. Until something is labeled as unusual, it remains normal.

I have come to understand that entertaining provided Mom with a circumscribed world that she could completely control, a common need for those suffering from the illness. Mom could not completely control the upkeep of the Castle. That required Helen, her decorator

Jerry, and a team of gardeners and handymen. She certainly could not control her three young children, each of us equipped with the potential for disrupting the best-laid plans.

But Mom could dictate every aspect of her parties. She decided who was to be invited, what time they arrived, how long to have cocktails, where everyone would sit, what dish to serve on which plates, and whether coffee was to be served at the table or in the living room. The parties also gave Mom an opportunity to pore over recipe books and talk endlessly to her friends about what had been served.

It was around this time that I began to notice Mom's obsession with food. Lacking a context in which to place it, I did not associate it with her illness. But from my perch at the kitchen table, I observed her slavishly copying down recipes from magazines, like some twelfth-century monk. She wrote them on file cards in her meticulous handwriting and stored them in a series of little, plastic boxes.

I also watched her fixate on certain foods. For example, she was obsessed with cheese and always kept a wooden tray with four or five rare, imported brands in the fridge. Cheese may have had an appeal because it is easy to consume in small quantities. Mom wielded a cheese knife to carve slices as thin as gossamer wings. Fat-free cottage cheese was another staple. She also liked to dip sliced-up pieces of celery, cauliflower, and broccoli into fat-free ranch dressing. Though she served us roast beef and steak for dinner, she gave herself only a piece of plain white fish, or a boneless, skinless chicken breast. I noticed all of these things, though it never registered as unusual.

Mom's friends did, however, notice a subtle change in her behavior. She had an unusually large number of friends, spanning all the way from her childhood in New York, to college friends at Wellesley, and new acquaintances from San Francisco. Before the onset of the illness, none of them could have predicted her anorexia nervosa.

But after Menninger, though she remained unusually empathetic and interested in the details of their lives, she was different. As one friend explained: "Carol had such a good mind that I couldn't guess what she was going to say next. It was always fun to talk with her. But after Menninger she was less spontaneous. She didn't glow and engage you in conversation quite as eagerly."

~

I'd grown accustomed to returning home from school and finding both Mom and Helen in the kitchen. Increasingly, I discovered Helen there alone. Though she greeted me the same, I began to worry.

"Where's Mom?" I would ask, watching Helen to gauge her reaction. If I saw her pause and scrunch up her face, I could already guess the news.

"Your mama's been to the dentist," Helen would respond, shaking her head. "Why don't you go upstairs and sit with her for a spell."

Although anorexia nervosa is classified as a mental illness, the Diagnostic and Statistical Manual of the American Psychiatric Association also describes related physical impacts that can occur. The potential problems, all resulting from semi-starvation, include anemia, impaired renal function, cardiovascular problems, osteoporosis, and dental problems.

As far as I knew, Mom's teeth had rebelled for unknown reasons. Even that early on, I had already spent too much time seeing her sick. It appeared to me that God was subjecting Mom to a series of plagues, like the ones imposed upon the Egyptians as we discussed each year at our Passover seder.

It was always a shock to see her after one of her dental procedures. She looked so tiny in the bed with the covers pulled up to her chin. "Hi Mom," I'd whisper, as she rolled her head toward me and tried to force a smile. It often came out as a grimace instead. Closing her eyes with the effort, she'd whisper, "How was school?" and I tried to tell her about my day, ignoring that the pain or painkillers made it difficult for her to pay attention.

"Can I get you anything?" I'd ask.

"Something to drink."

I reached over to the half-filled glass of Tab on her bedside table and held the straw to her mouth. When she had enough, she let the straw slip from her lips and shook her head. After I made conversation for a while, I told her that she needed rest, and left to begin my homework. But sometimes, instead of looking at my books, I stared out the bedroom window and wondered why it was that Mom had to endure so much suffering.

~

Mom had been home from Menninger for a year in the fall of 1974 when Dad called us into the library for a meeting. When he announced that she was returning to the hospital, the news blindsided me. I never imagined it could happen again.

Mom interrupted our stunned silence to add that this time she would be closer to home. "I'll be at a new eating disorders clinic at Stanford University in Palo Alto," she said.

I already knew, from attending Stanford football games with a friend, that Palo Alto was less than an hour drive from the Castle. "We'll be able to visit Mom often, and she'll be able to visit us," Dad said, as if this might cheer us up.

Unbeknownst to my brothers and me, Mom had already met with psychiatrists who were then in the process of establishing a new eating disorders clinic at the Stanford University School of Medicine.

Professors there had heard about the successes of applying behavioral techniques to anorexia nervosa and obesity. Because most of the results involved individuals or small groups of patients, the Stanford doctors decided to test the findings on a larger scale. They established a 20-bed clinic within the larger psychiatric hospital.

The program appealed to Dr. Jeff Pearson, a psychiatric resident, who was placed in charge of its development. Thirty years later, Dr. Pearson explained the pitch that had convinced him to take on the program. "The department head asked if I'd ever thought about fat," he began. "It's something tangible to study in this world of psychiatry. If you put someone on a scale they get fatter or thinner. It intrigued me because you can tell if the treatment was effective or not."

The Stanford psychiatrists explained the program to Mom, stressing that it was voluntary, and that it was her decision alone whether to participate. They described a system of punishments and rewards based on designated weight gain. Before exiting the clinic, a patient had to reach an agreed-upon target weight. As Mom later noted, the concreteness of the approach appealed to her. She agreed to begin the experimental program.

~

It was Tuesday evening, "Family Night," a group therapy session for patients and their families. Mom had urged my brothers and I to attend. We drove down from San Francisco in the late afternoon so we could have dinner with her before the session. With the exception of fleeting visits to Menninger, I had never spent time with Mom in a hospital setting before coming to Stanford.

The familiar smell of eucalyptus greeted us as we got out of the car and walked to the clinic building. Like Menninger, the Stanford campus was a bucolic and peaceful environment. With its mustard-colored buildings and red-tiled roofs, it conveyed the impression of a serene hacienda, an image enhanced by the oak and eucalyptus trees. Exiting the elevator on the second floor, I was struck by the pleasant, sterile atmosphere, more Holiday Inn than Mount Zion Hospital, where earlier in the year I'd had a benign tumor removed from my left arm. Unlike Mount Zion where the nurses all dressed in white, the Stanford nurses wore pastel blouses and blue or white pants.

"My three men," Mom exclaimed as soon as she saw us. She hugged us tightly and then proceeded to introduce us to everyone in the room. "These are my boys," she boasted, and we smiled and said hello as if greeting guests in our living room. The other patients were all young females, most seemed not much older than Jimmy's age of 18. At 44, Mom was by far the oldest person on the ward.

"Your mother is so wonderful," the women said, over and over. "She gives great advice and is so wise. We just love her." Mom beamed at their praise, as did I, happy that she was appreciated. I was not jealous that these strangers were benefiting from Mom's kindness and judgment, even while my brothers and I were going without her at home.

On this particular evening Mom was allowed to eat dinner with us. Under the clinic's rules she typically ate all meals alone in her room and had to sit with the food for at least 45 minutes whether she ate it or not. She liked eating alone. She harbored a terrible anxiety about putting a forkful of food in her mouth. Alone, in her room, she could pick up crumbs with her fingers.

Mom escorted us to the dining area where shafts of late after-noon light slipped in through the sliding glass doors. "I'll be back in a moment," she said, and disappeared into the kitchen to retrieve her dinner—a lonely slab of sauceless white fish and side dishes of dry lettuce and a mixture of steamed cauliflower, broccoli, and carrots. From her purse she extracted a silver-plated counter, similar to the ones used by baseball umpires to record balls and strikes.

"I have to keep track of the number of bites I eat at each meal," she explained, placing the counter next to the fish. "This way I know exactly how much I'm eating, kind of like a game." Sure enough, after she had placed a bite of food in her mouth and began chewing, she dutifully picked up the counter and gave it a firm press with her thumb.

The clicker was additional evidence of Mom's odd relationship with food. Before she left for Stanford, I had started to notice that when I awoke in the middle of the night, long after everyone had gone to bed, I would hear noises coming from the kitchen. I soon discovered that it was Mom who would stay down there until two or three in the morning doing who knows what. She already spent most of her days in the kitchen; it was hard to believe most of her nights were there too.

Mom had called with the invitation to Family Night a few days earlier, but had cautioned that she would not know until that morning whether she would be able to attend. Each morning a nurse came to Mom's door to escort her to the scale, the impartial arbiter of her day's fate. After donning a thin, cotton nightgown (the same one every day) and a brief stop at the bathroom for voiding (as it is known in the literature), Mom stood on the scale while the nurse recorded her weight on a clipboard. If she had gained one-half pound over the previous day, she could make phone calls, entertain visitors, even leave the hospital grounds to stroll across the street to the Stanford Shopping Center.

If the scale revealed that Mom had gained between a half pound and a quarter pound, she was free to wander about the clinic until noon, after which time she was confined to her room for the rest of the day and evening. In her room, she could read books, write, play games, or listen to the radio. If she had gained less than a quarter pound, Mom had to spend all day in her room with only a couple of five-minute breaks to prepare a snack in the kitchen. If she failed to achieve her goal for three straight days, the nurses were to remove all distractions, including reading materials and the radio. Because Mom had gained the requisite one-half pound on this particular Tuesday, there was no phone call telling us not to come.

After Mom finished her dinner and recorded the number of bites in a notebook, she took us to see her room. It was not particularly distinctive—a twin bed, a bedside table, a small desk and chair, a clock radio, curtains on the windows. Two pieces of butcher-block paper hung on the wall. On one, a graph showed a slow but steady upward trend, the record of Mom's daily weight gain. The other piece of paper was a traced outline of a woman's body.

"What's that?" I asked, pointing to the strange artwork.

"That's me," Mom replied. "We took turns tracing each other's body in an arts and crafts class."

Years later, Dr. JoEllen Werne, one of the clinic psychiatrists, reminded me of that traced image of Mom's body. "Many of these women had distorted views of themselves," Dr. Werne recalled. "Even though they were dangerously thin, they had the illusion they were fat. We had them trace their bodies and compare them to the traced bodies of the nurses to show them that they were indeed much thinner."

There are so many aspects of anorexia nervosa that are difficult to understand. But this is one of the hardest. How could anyone who weighed so little possibly think they looked fat? Some psychiatrists suggest that anorexic patients may suffer from a kind of psychosis, where there is a distortion of the person's ability to see their body realistically. As with all mental illnesses, it is almost impossible for the non-sick to comprehend what might be happening in the sick person's brain.

Someone had arranged the plastic chairs into a circle in the room where Family Night was to take place. A few patients were already there—thin, young women accompanied by parents, husbands, or siblings. Mom introduced us to anyone we might not yet have met, and then we assumed our seats on either side of her. I crossed and uncrossed my legs, attempting to get comfortable. I whispered jokes to John, trying to make him laugh. I did anything I could think of to distract myself from the prospect of having to talk about myself or my family in the presence of these strangers.

Other patients and family members continued to shuffle in, and I tried not to stare. While some appeared animated and interacted with their guests, others did not even acknowledge their relatives sitting next to them. At precisely 7 P.M., two people, a man and a woman, strode in the door and took a seat. They were young and carried clipboards and I was drawn to them, sensing that they were about to take charge and relieve some of the discomfort and tension.

"Welcome to Family Night," the male psychiatrist said. "I know that our patients appreciate your willingness to come here tonight to help in the process of their recovery. This is a safe environment where you can speak honestly about the feelings you may have about having a loved one in this clinic. Everything we say in here will be confidential, and we hope you will feel comfortable speaking your mind. Who would like to begin?"

A painful silence ensued and my eyes darted about the room to see if someone was going to raise their hand. Most of the other people stared at the floor or gazed into their coffee mugs. The sound of Mom clearing her throat broke the silence. "I'll begin," she said.

Mom's legs were crossed and she was hunched over, her back curved into a crescent as if she was trying to dissolve into herself. She spoke in a voice so muted I had to lean toward her in order to hear what she was saying.

"I'm really grateful," she began, "that my three boys made the trip down from San Francisco to be with me tonight. I'm so proud of them." And she looked at each of us and we smiled back, though I saw my own tension reflected in my brother's tight smiles. There was a long wait and when she continued, her voice had risen in pitch. "Sometimes," she said and paused. "Sometimes… when I think about my family… I feel like I've let everybody down." She hesitated again. "I mean, I've been away from home so much and I've tried to get better but it just seems so hard."

Her voice trailed off and was replaced with a soft wail, watered with tears. "I feel like I've been a terrible wife and mother," she said, and then her voice dissolved into crying.

I knew I should feel sorry for Mom. Instead, I felt empty, shut down, like a sea anemone that has been poked and balls up into itself. If I felt anything, it was embarrassment at this public airing of emotion. We didn't know these people, yet here was Mom, crying and "carrying on," as Helen might have said. I wanted to disappear, fall down a hole somewhere, but there was no escape.

Mom was unable to continue. The psychiatrist addressed my brothers and me. "Would any of you boys care to respond?" he asked. "Do any of you feel that your mother has let you down in some way? Be honest here."

I held my breath, waiting for John or Jimmy to say something. I certainly wasn't going to be the first to talk. Besides, what could I say? I knew not to mention anything that might further upset Mom, which basically ruled out honesty. And even if I had the courage or ability to be honest, I didn't have any idea what impact her illness or prolonged absences might have had on me. For all I knew, we were a happy family with one atypical feature—that Mom was sick and had to go away, sometimes for long periods of time. Nobody acknowledged that this was unusual or made us special in any way.

John broke the silence. "I think Mom has been a wonderful mother, and I don't feel she has let us down at all. I'm just sorry she has been sick and has had to be away from home so much."

Jimmy agreed. "Mom is my best friend. I feel like I can talk to her about anything."

"I agree with what my brothers have said," I chimed in.

Mom's sniffling receded and she looked up at us with a sheepish smile. I imagined what the other patients and their families must have been saying to themselves: What a wonderful family. Why can't we be more like that? Equilibrium, that treasured state in which feelings never get too messy or out of control, had been restored.

Instead, it was the other families who were less poised, and whom I saw as embarrassing themselves. In hindsight, they were probably doing something we could have used—expressing their pain.

"You're damn right I'm angry at my daughter," said one father to the psychiatrist, while his waif-like daughter slumped in her chair. "I think she is doing this just to get back at my wife and I, to punish us for somehow not being good enough parents. It's ironic, because we've done everything for her—good schools, paid for all her various lessons—and this is how she repays us."

The psychiatrist addressed the daughter: "Are you doing this to get back at your parents?"

"They never listen," she said dejectedly. "They have no idea how I'm feeling. I'm not doing this to get back at anyone. I just can't seem to help it."

I looked between the despondent girl and her father. Why doesn't he listen to her? I asked myself. She is so obviously helpless.

~

After two months at Stanford, Mom reached her weight goal of 110 pounds and returned home from the clinic. Six months later she agreed to an interview with a *San Francisco Chronicle* reporter who had heard about her situation. Mom explained that since leaving Stanford her weight had stayed between 106 and 110 pounds, she had started to take secretarial courses in the hope of finding a job, and most important, she could for the first time speak openly about her illness. Given the silence that continued to surround the anorexia at home, I was surprised she would speak so easily to a stranger about it.

"I don't think it will happen again," Mom told the interviewer. "But I also think I'll never not have a problem with food. It's like somebody who has been on drugs. Eating is difficult for me."

She paused before making her final point, "But after all, you have to eat to live."

6

DESCENT

According to Jewish tradition, the Bar Mitzvah signals the passage into manhood. I had looked forward to the recognition of my 13th year after enduring each of my brother's celebrations. In the midst of their luncheons that included laughter, conversation, and clinking glasses, I had quietly calculated the number of years until, as the Bar Mitzvah boy, I would assume my rightful position at the center of attention.

Mine was everything I had expected—I was showered with gifts, including a Webster's Dictionary and a Roget's Thesaurus from

Mom and Dad that remain on my desk. But when I feel the cool leather of the dictionary against my palm, I realize that it is neither the attention, nor the gifts, nor the spiritual significance that makes my Bar Mitzvah a happy memory. Instead, it is the knowledge that not long afterward something broke in me, a feeling of optimism and hope that could never quite be recovered.

Dressed in a jacket and green and white polka dot tie, I stand next to Mom in a photograph taken that day. It's the last picture I own of her that does not cause me to shudder. She'd been home for six months and she certainly looked healthy. In the picture, Mom's head is perched on my right shoulder as she stands in a light pink sweater with a blouse of green and white to match my suit. Despite the many fluctuations in her weight, her skin remained smooth, her face nicely filled out, and she looked younger than her 45 years. Anyone observing her would have had difficulty noticing something was wrong.

Earlier in the day Mom had lit the Sabbath candles, as is traditional, at the Temple. Though this was her third time, she'd practiced reciting the prayers at home throughout the preceding week. When she'd arisen to light the candles, I watched nervously, afraid that she might make a mistake. Though her voice quavered and her hands shook a little while holding the match, she perfectly fulfilled the role.

I have sometimes wondered whether Mom's feelings about Judaism were enhanced by connections she made between her religion and a time in her life before she fell ill. In the small town of Woodmere, New York, she lived in a Jewish household and a Jewish community, surrounded by Jewish friends. There was never any question that she would marry a Jewish husband. Though she had many Jewish friends in San Francisco, it was not a way of life for most people. Perhaps the rituals of purchasing a challah, a round egg bread for Friday night dinner, or preparing apples and honey for Rosh Hashanah, the Jewish New Year, took her back to when the future, and all of its possibilities, danced in front of her.

Sitting in the Temple now, did she ask God what had happened?

~

The biggest Bar Mitzvah present I received was a trip to the East Coast. Three weeks of visiting relatives would be the longest and farthest I had been away from home by myself.

My first night sleeping in Grandma and Grandpa B.'s apartment on 36th Street in Manhattan, something strange happened. Earlier in the evening, Grandpa had taken me to Grand Central's famous Oyster Bar, where we'd eaten clam chowder, a bucketful of steamed clams, and a full, spiny lobster that Grandpa dismembered with a silver nutcracker. The feast was topped off with slices of buttery-soft cheesecake. It was the best meal I had ever eaten.

But that night, lying in the foldout bed in my grandparent's spare bedroom, I felt disconnected. As I stared out at the lights of the city and listened to the muffled sounds of car horns and sirens, I longed for my bed at home. Something inside of me wished for the mournful wail of the foghorns, for the blinking red lights of the television tower on Mount Sutro, and for the reassuring sound of KCBS anchorman Dave McElhatton delivering "traffic and weather together every 20 minutes" on my clock radio.

Each night during my trip, despite the days packed with activity, I felt lonely and miserable. It wasn't until I arrived in Boston that my Aunt Lois diagnosed my malaise. "Sounds like you're a little bit homesick," she said. So much for becoming a man, I thought.

Maybe, at some level, I hated to be away from the Castle when Mom was home and seemed to be doing so well. Upon returning in August, I spent many afternoons in the library, listening to albums I received for my Bar Mitzvah: the Rolling Stones' *It's Only Rock and Roll* and Elton John's *Goodbye Yellow Brick Road.* I studied the Elton John songs until I could recite them by heart.

In early September, just before I began eighth grade, Dad called us into the library. Jimmy had already left for the University of California at Davis, so it was just the four of us. In the sad voice I had come to know so well, Dad said that Mom was returning to Stanford for more treatment.

While I readied myself to go to a private high school and Mom prepared to leave home, I continued to listen to the Elton John album, in particular the title song, "Goodbye Yellow Brick Road." I couldn't stop singing one line in particular: *Well I finally decided my future lies beyond the yellow brick road.*

~

Nine months later, my eighth grade graduation party unfolded in Sausalito, a Mediterranean-like village across the Golden Gate Bridge from San Francisco. It was 1976, and the distance I had traveled from childhood was about to be made abundantly clear. Hunting for the bathroom, I accidentally opened a bedroom door and was engulfed in thick, pungent smoke. Several of the cooler kids from my class were scattered around the room. I noticed, but chose to ignore, the hostile looks some of them shot my way. Instead I planted myself, waiting for the joint to make its way around the room.

I had smoked pot before, as early as the sixth grade with Jimmy at Lake Tahoe. Despite my striving to feel "high," nothing had ever happened. This particular night I took a deep hit of the joint and coughed so emphatically that I thought a lung might burst. Once I regained my breath, I noticed a pleasant dizziness and a tingling in my fingertips. I tried to explain what I was experiencing to my smirking classmates, but each time I opened my mouth I dissolved into a fit of giggles.

I wandered out on the deck and danced through the crowd, rolling my shoulders to Van Morrison's "Brown-Eyed Girl." Whenever I saw one of my friends, I grabbed their arms and blubbered, "You are so great." I was like the one person at every wedding who has discovered alcohol for the first time. I didn't care what anyone thought.

In retrospect, the timing was ripe for my descent into drugs. Jimmy was gone, Mom spent several months back at Stanford, and John was busy serving as the student body president of his high school. Dad was often out in the evenings and on weekends and busied himself in the library when he was home. I seemed to be the only one without anything to do.

Everything conspired to fuel my addiction. My bedroom was a perfect place to hide and smoke. It had originally been built for a girl, opening into a dressing room that led into a bathroom. Three doors thus separated the bathroom from the hallway. I developed a routine. First, I stuck my head in the hallway to see if anyone was nearby. Then I would stand at the head of the stairs, gauging what was happening in the kitchen. If I smelled turkey gravy or shrimp gumbo, I knew Helen was busy; Cigarette smoke meant she was on the phone and would be occupied. If Mom and Helen were both in the kitchen and their voices were raised, I knew an argument could break out any time, and Mom might suddenly bolt upstairs. If Mom was alone, she could stay in the kitchen all day.

Once I gave myself the all clear, I put a record on the stereo—David Bowie's "Young Americans" or anything by the Grateful

Dead—and locked myself in the bathroom. I sat on the blue-tiled floor, rested my back against the glass shower door, and faced the window just above the bathtub. The toilet, just on the left, made a perfect ashtray. When I first began smoking, I could fully extend my legs between the shower and the bathtub; as high school went on, my knees kept rising higher, like little hills.

I smoked joints, which I prepared with a plastic rolling machine that resembled a child's toy. I'd suck on the joint until my chest expanded with smoke, then extinguish the little orange ember with my thumb and forefinger. To this day, the tips of those fingers remain numb from repeated burnings. After holding in the hit for as long as possible, I blew out the smoke, like the tailings from a tiny jet, toward the open window

Home alone one night, I was excited at the prospect of getting stoned by myself and watching my favorite lineup of Thursday evening shows. I flicked on the television at 8 P.M. to catch the opening credits for *One Day at a Time*, starring Valerie Bertinelli, whom I'd long held a crush on. I admired Valerie's level-headedness compared to her crazy family, not to mention her feathered hair, pug nose, and brown eyes. As the program unfolded, I thought that if I could just meet Valerie in person, sit down and really talk with her, surely she would like me. Maybe, she might even want to be my girlfriend. Alas, by 8:30, she was gone.

At one point the phone rang and I went out into the hallway to answer it. On the other end was Julie, a girl from school, whom I had gone to dinner with a few weeks earlier—my first real date. The evening had been a disaster. I spent most of the meal wondering how to pay the check without revealing the $50 bill Dad had let me borrow. Surely she would know I didn't just carry around $50 bills. I paid while she was in the bathroom. Then I kept refilling her teacup, not knowing what to do next. Finally, she suggested we walk up to Coit Tower to look at the view. Standing with the lights of San Francisco sparkling below, I wanted to kiss her. Paralyzed with fear and indecision, I barely looked her way.

Now, almost two weeks later, she was on the phone.

"My family and I are going skiing tomorrow," she said brightly, "and I just wanted to call and say hello before we left."

"You ski?" I asked.

"Yes, I love to ski. Do you?"

"Uh, no, I don't ski."

My shyness around girls was made a hundred times worse by the pot. Topics popped into my head, but I immediately analyzed and discarded them as too trite or awkward. Julie tried a couple more times to ignite a conversation. Each time, I replied in monosyllables.

"Well, I guess I'll be seeing you," she said.

"Yeah, see you," I replied, instead wanting to plead: "Please don't go; maybe we could get together again sometime." After she hung up, I just sat there listening to the dial tone.

I returned to the bathroom for a few more hits of pot. I tried to lose myself again in the television, but my mind kept returning to the aborted conversation. If only I hadn't been stoned, I thought. I might have been able to talk to her.

Looking back, I wish I'd taken that lesson to heart. This was a crossroads and choosing the path of getting high was not the best way to fend off those feelings—sadness, loneliness—that had started to take hold. What I needed instead, I now realize, was a deeper connection to the people I loved, beginning with Mom and Dad. But they were unavailable, so I filled in their absence on the bathroom floor.

Years later, I came across an article in which Julie, who went on to become a successful writer, recounted her teenaged battle with anorexia nervosa. I eventually dated several women who revealed they had struggled with eating disorders. It was surprising to realize that my attraction to such women had started as early as my first date.

～

On high school weekends, I usually went out to get stoned with friends. No matter what time I returned home, even if was after midnight, I'd find Mom in the kitchen, as if she was haunting it. She would be there dressed in her white, terrycloth bathrobe, padding around.

The first few times, I cursed my bad luck, certain she would notice my bloodshot eyes, or the reek of marijuana on my clothes. But it soon became apparent that she either didn't care or was too preoccupied to notice. While I took my place at the table, eyes half open and head drooping, she would root around in the fridge and extract a tub of nonfat cottage cheese. Then she would head to the toaster oven to heat up pieces of French bread crust she had scraped clean of the white part. While we chatted, she nibbled on mouse-sized pieces of crust dipped shallowly into the cottage cheese. Watching her, I remembered the ice cream sundae I had devoured earlier at the Chocolate Factory at Ghirardelli Square.

I wondered why Mom was always in the kitchen no matter what time I came home. Soon, like everything else, it became a normal part of the landscape. It was many years after her death, after reading the *Chronicle* interview about the terror she experienced in raising a forkful of food to her mouth, that I understood the odd hours of the night was her time to eat whatever and however she chose. Those late nights in the kitchen kept her alive.

Just as food had become Mom's coping mechanism for whatever was not working in her life, so marijuana had become mine. The two of us spent many nights reaching out awkwardly to each other across the chasm of our obsessions. Even though these conversations were stilted, at least we both tried. By contrast, my association with Dad at the time could be captured in an image: The two of us sitting silently in his car.

Dad sold his shoe business while I was finishing elementary school and wound up buying and fixing up small shopping centers. They were all located outside of San Francisco and sometimes, on the weekends, he asked me to accompany him. In spite of my growing loneliness at home, I dreaded these invitations because Dad and I had nothing to say to each other. In the car, as the silence grew thicker and heavier, my mind raced to come up with topics of mutual interest. When I did think of something—asking him to explain how a lease worked or commenting on the state of relations in the Middle East—the resulting conversation was stilted, and I stumbled, as if trying to ask a girl out. The silence fertilized my mind, which began to grow in uncomfortable directions: *Why aren't Dad and I closer? My other friends seem to have good relationships with their fathers. Is there something wrong with me?* I'm not sure why I blamed myself for the lowly state of our relations; perhaps it was the easiest thing to do.

~

Twice more, in April 1978 and June 1980, Mom returned to Stanford for three-month stints of treatment. Meanwhile, the Castle grew even quieter with John's departure for Vassar College in the summer of 1978. Though John and I spent little time together, I hadn't realized until he was gone how much I valued his presence down the hall. After Mom and Dad left the Castle to drive him to the airport, I sat on the white couch in my bedroom, staring out the window. I felt utterly alone and abandoned.

Not long after John left, Dad told me one evening that he wanted to chat in the library. He sat in his black Eames chair and packed tobacco into his pipe, while my eyes darted nervously at the face-down report card on the chair's armrest. He cleaned the pipe stem with a wire pipe cleaner, lit a match, and drew the flame into the tobacco with a few deep sucks. He then waved the match out, picked up the report card, and looked at me.

"Have you seen your report card for this quarter?" he asked, holding the document by his fingertips as if it might be toxic.

"I know I didn't do as well as I could have," I muttered.

"These grades make me wonder whether Mom and I are wasting our money sending you to private school. If your grades don't start improving, our only option will be to send you to public school."

I decided that this was a good time to raise an issue I had been thinking about since John's departure.

"You know," I mumbled, "I've had this thought that maybe boarding school might be a good idea."

This caught Dad off guard.

"Boarding school? Why in the world do you want to go to boarding school?"

"I don't know; it just seems like it might be a good thing to do."

Dad's face softened as he puffed on his pipe. When he spoke again, his tone was less stern. "I don't think boarding school is going to help your grades. You just need to buckle down and work a little harder. You want to go to college, don't you?"

I nodded.

"Well, if you don't get better grades, you may have a hard time getting in where you want to go. Boarding school isn't the answer."

As bad as I wanted a break from the Castle, I did not have much of an argument for boarding school and could not convince Dad.

Instead I continued to seek escape in marijuana and my imagination. Since Jimmy was away at college, I was free to rummage around in his room. I discovered his stash of underground ZAP comic books, which transported me to a world that I longed to inhabit: a place where hippies passed their time smoking dope, having sex, and flaunting authority.

After my disastrous encounter with Julie, I had had no other dates in high school. Instead, ZAP comics taught me everything I knew about sex, which wasn't much. I read about the exploits of Wonder Wart Hog, the Fabulous Furry Freak Brothers, and Mr. Natural. Because the Freak Brothers lived in a state of bohemian squalor, I suggested to Helen that she stop cleaning up my room.

"Boy," she said. "You're sure going to have to take that up with your Daddy." I let the idea drop.

~

During a trip to Great Britain the next summer, I was relieved to exchange the Castle's quiet for the constant companionship of my best friend, Martin, several kids from the neighborhood, and a teacher whom I had known for almost a decade. It was liberating to be so far from home, and unlike the excursion I'd taken to the East Coast, this trip was not laced with homesickness.

It wasn't until the plane ride home that I noticed something amiss. As the plane descended into a late-afternoon fog that had settled over San Francisco, I became anxious, seized by an instinctive, guttural instinct to flee, to go anywhere else but home. Of course, I had nowhere to go.

Because Mom and Dad were out of town, one of my tripmates' parents drove me to the Castle. I recall standing outside the metallic garage doors, unable to push the numbers on the keypad to let myself in the back door.

I wonder now: Was this the way Mom felt that first time she came back from Menninger? As if she was returning to a life against her will? Perhaps, like me, the thought of coming home filled her with dread, even if she couldn't explain why.

Lugging my suitcase, I climbed the back stairs and entered the kitchen, where I was greeted with the aroma of roasting turkey and a vision of Helen bending over the stove.

"Hi Helen," I said in a barely audible voice.

She looked up. "Daniel, we been expecting you boy. Come over here and let me take a look at you. You're looking skinny, boy. Did those people give you enough to eat?"

I nodded, giving her a weak hug.

"It's almost dinnertime and Mr. Jimmy is upstairs sleeping, lazy boy. Go wake him up."

My heart lifted a little; perhaps seeing Jimmy would help me regain my balance. Although he had been away at college, Jimmy and I had grown closer over the previous year. The University of California at Davis was only 90 miles from San Francisco. When he came down to visit, the two of us smoked pot in his room. I was thrilled that my brother—"a real hippie"—according to my friends, was all of a sudden paying attention to me.

I went up to his room where he was asleep on the bed. I shook him awake as he rolled over and caught a glimpse of me. "Danny Boy," he said. "How's it going? Want to get stoned?"

He reached under his bed and slid out a record album with a couple of joints lying on top. He lit one up and handed it over.

Thanks to my one-month abstinence, the pot went straight to my head. Dizzy, I sat down for fear of falling over.

Jimmy smiled. "Pretty good stuff, huh?" I wiped the tears from my eyes and nodded.

"Dinner!" Helen yelled. Jimmy slipped the album back under the bed and handed me a breath mint. We went downstairs to the table where I stared at my plate of food: turkey, dressing, mashed potatoes, stuffing. I had no appetite. The pot enhanced the despair engulfing me. Something was seriously wrong.

The telephone interrupted my thoughts. Helen burst out of the back bedroom. "You boys keep your butts at the table. I'll answer it."

She spoke in the receiver,

"Mr. Becker, how ya doin'? Fine, fine. Yeah he made it home. He's right here."

I was in no state of mind to talk to Mom and Dad, but there was no way to avoid it. I rose from the table and moved toward the phone as if heading for my own execution. I took a deep breath, trying to sound calm.

"Hi Dad."

"Hi Daniel. How was your trip?"

"Great, great. I had a really nice time."

There was a long pause. *I haven't seen him a month and still I have nothing to say. What is wrong with me?*

Dad's voice took on a stern tone. "You know, we only received two letters from you. How come you didn't write more or call us?"

Though I couldn't think of a response, my mind wasn't quiet. Dad had hit on an essential truth: I hadn't thought much about my parents while I was away. But now thoughts about them came rushing into my head.

What kind of son goes away for a whole month and doesn't think about his parents? How selfish and ungrateful can I possibly be? Don't I know they have problems, that they are suffering?

"Here's your mother."

Mom's voice was softer. She asked for details about the trip, being the good cop. But it was too late. My mind, moving down a path of guilt and despair, was no longer listening. I felt like a jockey, sitting atop a horse over which I had no control, forced along for the ride no matter where we ended up.

"You know, I'm really tired," I said, interrupting her. "I think I need to go to sleep."

"OK sweetheart. We'll see you in a couple of days."

I hung up, excused myself from the table, and went upstairs to lie down. My head was spinning from the pot but there was something else: a feeling of emptiness so deep it scared me.

What is happening to me? When will this feeling go away?

It carried on for weeks, then months. I had trouble sleeping, waking up at odd hours in the night sweating and panicked. I shuffled through my days, listless and sad. Because I could not explain what I was experiencing, I kept it all to myself. Smoking pot provided temporary relief. But whenever the high wore off, I plummeted into even deeper despair.

I spent hours staring at the vanity mirror in my dressing room, wondering if I was going crazy. Whenever I tried to type a paper for school, my fingers automatically typed out the word *sadness*.

When I was with other people, I felt like my previous self. I told jokes, earned mediocre grades, played on the soccer and basketball teams, wrote for the school newspaper. But when I was alone, which happened more and more frequently, nothing could check the expansion of that compartment inside of me that housed my despair. After several months, I realized I was never going back to my old self. I smoked ever more pot, even experimented with stronger drugs, but it only made matters worse. I spent more and more time alone, hiding from Mom, Dad, and Helen so they wouldn't discover me stoned. As the gap widened between the self I exhibited to the world and the hidden self I kept inside, I worried that I might split apart.

Typically, a depression like this can be attributed to a specific experience, or perhaps the hormones of adolescence. My explanation at the time was that it was punishment for being a bad son and leading an increasingly dissolute life. The fact that I had left for the summer and hardly thought about Mom and Dad was proof of my ungratefulness; the fact that I smoked so much pot and still felt awful was further evidence that my unhappiness resulted from bad character.

Perhaps my depression was a way to remain loyal to Mom and Dad. After all, what could have been more disloyal than my remaining happy while I knew they were suffering? Maybe I was seeking some way to attach, to not feel left out. Or was it even more direct? Did Mom unknowingly implant me with some of the same faulty genes that contributed to her anorexia nervosa? Scientists have now proven that depression can be passed along in families. Maybe I had no choice.

7

PORTRAIT

I first began to understand something about Mom's illness during the years between John's departure for college and my own. Not that anyone said anything. Whenever Mom went back to the hospital, it was because she was "sick and needed to get better." Dad never sat me down to explain what that sickness was or that it had something to do with an eating disorder. Talking about it with Mom, I knew, was strictly off limits.

This was in 1978, when Mom and Dad decided to take the family to France. The trip was arranged around main courses that

Mom would never eat—lobster at a restaurant in Rouen, the omelets at a brasserie in Mont St. Michelle. Planning the trip involved Mom scribbling notes from the green Guide Michelin, the bible of French restaurant reviews, then cross-checking the list against the hundreds of reviews she had collected over the years in manila file folders. Next she interrogated her friends for feedback about the restaurants, as if she was a lawyer who needing to get the facts just right. Questions such as what they had ordered and if they had enjoyed their meals were important.

On this trip I became fully aware of Mom's odd behavior in restaurants. As soon as a waiter appeared, she would dig into him. "What kind of sauce does the duck come in? Is there dressing on the salad? Is the fish filleted in butter?" (While this behavior doesn't seem quite as odd given the ubiquity of all the diets out there today, then it was unheard of.)

She could never order anything as it was presented, always asking it to be prepared differently. The waiters usually looked mortally offended. My brothers and I hid behind our menus.

But that wasn't the end of it. No matter what the kitchen came up with, there was a problem. Usually Mom sent the food back. Sometimes she said "forget it" and left her plate untouched. In retrospect, she needed to be in complete control of her food, which was impossible in a restaurant. I never understood then why she loved to go out to eat so much.

After barely touching lunch one afternoon, Mom made selections from the cheese tray proffered at the conclusion of each French meal. Jimmy and John had already disappeared from the table, no doubt relieved to have escaped another too-long meal in a too-fancy restaurant.

"You really should try this one," Mom said, pointing to a

Camembert from which she had taken the tiniest of nibbles. "It's out of this world."

"I don't want any more cheese," I said, surprised at the sharp tone of my voice. I hadn't realized just how sick of the whole trip I had become. In contrast to our European tour six years earlier, the forces pulling us apart had multiplied. In the center of it all was Mom and her increasing obsession. The more she talked about food, the more withdrawn the rest of us became, as if we were busy trying to digest all the meals she ordered but never ate.

Despite my refusal, Mom picked up the piece of cheese and plopped it down on my plate. Without thinking, I grabbed it and half-threw it back on hers.

"I told you I didn't want it."

I knew immediately that I had crossed a boundary. I stared at Mom's plate, not believing what I had just done. For a moment, time stopped. Then things happened quickly. Mom's chair scraped against the wood floor. Her face scrunched in a spasm of agony. She began to cry, her voice making an ululating sound, like the Moslem call to prayer. I had heard her make this sound only once before on Family Night.

"I'm sorry," she sputtered. "I know I'm a burden to all of you. I just can't help myself. I hate it, I hate it."

Then she was gone, running across the room and up the stairs that led to the hotel's bedrooms. The sound of her voice echoed in the silent room.

I stared down at my plate. I tried to say something, but my voice dissolved into sobs. Dad placed his hand on top of mine. "It's not your fault," he said. "You didn't do anything wrong."

"I didn't mean to do it," I blurted. "It just happened."

"I know. It's understandable."

We sat in silence for a few moments. I breathed deeply a couple of times to gain control of my voice.

"I don't know how you do it," I said to Dad. "You guys eat dinner out all the time. How can you stand it? Watching her play with her food. How rude she is to waiters."

"It's very hard," he said. "Believe me, I understand."

At that moment, staring down at a piece of runny cheese, his hand resting on top of mine, I felt closer to Dad than I could ever remember. For once, conversation did not seem necessary. We were in a comfortable silence, both of us connected.

Dad rose from the table. "I better go see about Mom," he said.

That afternoon, Mom and I apologized to each other. Order was restored. I resolved to better control my behavior in the future. Years later, I heard depression described as anger channeled against one's self. Just for a moment, I had allowed my building anger toward Mom to seep out. The results had been disastrous. I vowed to not let it happen again.

~

Back home, despite her preoccupation with food, Mom remained keenly interested in our lives. She still demonstrated an uncanny ability to elicit from me even the most private information. Her natural empathy had been supplemented by the time spent with other patients at Menninger and Stanford. There was little that could shock her, little that she hadn't heard before.

Mom came to fetch me one day after I had had my wisdom teeth extracted. The dentist, having doped me up, wanted an hour to pass before clearing me to leave. Mom and I sat in the waiting room, apparently chatting away in spite of my cheeks stuffed with cotton. With no recollection of what we had discussed, I later asked Mom about it.

"Let's see," she began, matter-of-factly, "you said that you were worried about smoking too much pot and wanted to cut back."

Alarmed, I scanned her face for disapproval. Finding none, my attitude changed to annoyance. "It wasn't fair for you to ask me about drugs while I was in that condition."

"I never said a word," she replied, chuckling. "You just blurted it out."

Mom talked easily about topics I could never imagine discussing with Dad. Once, she brought up the new therapy group she had joined after leaving Stanford for the second time.

"The therapist asked everyone in the group to take turns sharing something they were particularly proud of. One guy mentioned his homegrown marijuana, so we all went over to his house and sat in his hot tub while he passed around a marijuana cigarette."

"Did you try some?" I asked, breathlessly.

"No," she replied, "I'm afraid to drink or take drugs. But I sat with them in the hot tub while everyone tried it, and they all seemed to be having a good time." She paused. "People are always telling me that I should try smoking pot because it might increase my appetite. They say it gives you the munchies."

At that moment, I was sure I had the coolest Mom in the world.

But it was rare to capture Mom's undivided attention. Whenever we chatted, she was invariably doing a number of things at the same time: clipping newspaper articles for friends, bickering with Helen, rummaging through the fridge, preparing grocery lists or invitation lists or lists of errands to run. I could only seem to make her focus on me if I was having a problem.

And I was having plenty of problems during those last years of high school. I was frequently cited for violating the school's policy against leaving campus, driving to Taco Bell to smoke pot and eat lunch with my friends. Finally, the school's administration sent a letter to Mom and Dad explaining that I had been placed on probation and that with one more violation, I would be expelled. Dad had already given me the public school talk and that remained his overriding threat. Mom decided to try a softer approach.

She suggested the two of us have lunch downtown at one of her favorite restaurants, the Iron Horse. The lighting was dim, and the other diners, divided between businessmen in suits and ladies carrying shopping bags, huddled and spoke in hushed tones, as if negotiating a business deal or swapping tidbits of gossip. It was the kind of place Mom's father had taken her when she was a child and he worked in Manhattan's Garment District.

Mom and I each chose the usual entrees—for her, a Caesar salad which she rarely actually ate, and a can of Tab. For me, a sirloin steak smothered in mushroom gravy. After handing the waiter my menu, I discovered Mom gazing at me with a big smile. "You love that sirloin steak don't you?" she asked. The thought of other people eating, particularly me, seemed to delight her.

"Now honey," Mom began, while reaching for a sourdough roll, "we need to talk about what has been going on at school."

While she talked, she dug her fingertips into the roll, picking off little pieces of crust and popping them into her mouth. I fixated on the growing pile of brown crumbs that accumulated in front of her on the white tablecloth. Periodically, when the pile grew big enough, she swept the crumbs into the palm of her hand and tilted them onto her bread plate.

"You know, Dad is very concerned about your situation. He doesn't want to see you get kicked out of school."

"Neither do I," I said, and meant it. I was terribly afraid of getting expelled. For one thing, I feared Dad's reaction. For another, college remained the Holy Grail, the solution to all my problems, and I did not have an alternative plan should that path suddenly be blocked. "I will be extra careful to follow all the rules," I said. "I know I can do it."

I was gripped by a desire to open up to Mom, to share with her the feelings about how awful I felt and what a bad person I was, and how I worried that there was something seriously wrong with me. That maybe I was going insane or something. I didn't know how to begin; I had no idea what words to use.

Instead, I watched her fiddle with her now almost-crustless roll, which looked naked and vulnerable, like a newborn baby chick.

The waiter returned and with a flourish placed Mom's salad in front of her. He was about to ask whether she wanted a few twists from a large pepper grinder when she grabbed the plate and held it back up.

"I asked for the dressing on the side," she said. "I can't eat it like this. Please take it back and bring me one with the dressing on the side."

"Madame," he began, " I don't recall that you asked for the dressing on the side, but if that is..."

"I did order it on the side," Mom interrupted. "I always ask for it on the side."

I was surprised by the rude tone in Mom's voice, although I'd seen similar performances. I swiveled my head from side to side, anxious to see if anyone was looking at us. By habit, I slid a little lower in my chair.

The waiter hesitated just long enough to register his annoyance. "Very well, Madame." He grasped the salad, pirouetted neatly, and disappeared.

I stared at my sirloin steak, unable to look up.

"Go ahead," Mom said cheerily, as if nothing had happened. "Don't wait for me."

Why does she do that? I wondered to myself. She isn't even going to eat it. If Mom noticed that for the rest of the meal I only spoke in monosyllables, "yes" or "no," she didn't let on. I hated my rudeness, but I couldn't shake off the funk that had suddenly descended. As she drove us back to the Castle after lunch, I sat sullenly in the passenger seat. I just need to get out of here, I said over and over to myself. I just have to hang on.

~

That summer, after my high school graduation, Mom and Dad had planned to take the family on a rafting trip down the Colorado River. Though by this time my brothers and I dreaded most family vacations, we looked forward to this one. Perhaps it was because we knew there would be no restaurants. Or maybe it was Mom's excitement as she reminisced about her summer camp experiences. I tried to picture Mom swimming, canoeing, playing tennis, horseback riding, and climbing mountains. It wasn't easy.

As late as my Bar Mitzvah in 1975, Mom was still beautiful. But by the time I graduated from high school four years later, Mom's anorexia nervosa had settled over her like a snowfall. The skin on her face had retracted, revealing cheek and jaw bones. Her eyes, still a lovely blue, gazed out from deep within their sockets above cheeks that were dotted with two dark spots, as if deliberately being sucked in. Even a casual glance at a photograph reveals that something is wrong.

At a fundraising auction for my old elementary school, she purchased a self-portrait to be painted by a well-regarded artist. It took Mom several years to get around to sitting for the portrait, but she finally posed in 1978. After the painting was finished, Mom took one look and sent it back. Though she looked pretty to me, the portrait had captured her drawn skin and puckered cheeks. "It doesn't look like me," Mom said flatly when I asked her why she didn't want the painting. The unclaimed canvas remained in the artist's basement for 25 years.

Maybe because I saw her everyday, I didn't notice the changes in her. So it was particularly upsetting when in May of 1980, Mom announced that she was returning to Stanford's eating disorders clinic. It was less than one month before the rafting trip and three months before I would leave for college. As with so many other family events, Mom would miss out on camping, the rest of us going without her.

Mom's hospitalization hung over my departure for college. Just as I was about to make my symbolic break with the past and all that it represented, I was pulled back. Once again, I was left to wonder why Mom and Dad had to endure so much sadness.

~

I applied to several colleges on the East Coast, desperate to go as far away as possible and begin a new life. Each day, I phoned home from school to see if any word had come from the admissions offices. One day, my Aunt Lois, visiting from Boston, picked up the phone. I asked if I had received any mail.

"An envelope came for you today from Dartmouth College." She paused dramatically. "It's thick."

I heard Mom shouting something in the background. "Do you

want us to open it?" Aunt Lois asked. "Yes," I said, and gripped the phone while she ripped the packet open. She began to read.

"Congratulations on being accepted to the Class of 1984."

Mom got on the phone. "Congratulations Daniel Boone," she cried. "I'm so proud of you."

I thought about those Saturday nights home alone when I had nothing better to do and had smoked in my bathroom. I'd often thought about my classmates and how much easier their lives seemed. It made me wonder what terrible thing I had done to bring so much unhappiness upon myself. During those times, only one idea separated me from hopelessness: college.

Now I felt as if I had been thrown a life rope from the future. Like something precious and vulnerable, I had nurtured the idea that everything would be better after I left for school—that whatever it was that made things so awful would melt away. Perhaps I should have realized my dream was constructed on a shaky foundation. But it was all I had.

8

DISAPPEAR

By the time I arrived at Dartmouth, it was too late at night to get into my dorm. So, I took a room in White River Junction, Vermont, chilled by the thought: *Nobody in the entire world except maybe the desk clerk knows where I am.* This place was nothing like the New York City Port Authority where I had boarded the bus almost ten hours earlier. There I had edged my way through the crowd, imbued with the fear Grandma B. had instilled in me. "Remember not to look up at the skyscrapers," she had warned. "They'll know you're an out-of-towner."

The next morning I would find my room on the third floor of the Richardson dormitory. It was already filled with cardboard boxes of books and clothes and a few scattered cups of a viscous brown liquid. I tried to guess what my roommates would be like from their stuff. I had asked for a nonsmoking room, the first step in my transformation from pot head to successful Ivy League student. I noticed several cigarette butts in an ashtray on the mantelpiece.

"Hey, you must be Daniel," said a voice behind me, and I wheeled to get a glimpse of my roommate, Eric, with telltale red eyes. "This place is totally awesome," he said. "I've been partying ever since I got here. Do you smoke weed?"

While the two of us sat on the floor and took hits from Eric's purple bong, I confessed that I had asked for a non-smoking room. He held up a finger at me while sucking in a giant hit, held it deep in his lungs, and dissolved in a fit of coughing. He finally caught his breath. "Me too!" he gasped.

"Hey, what is that stuff?" I asked, pointing to the cups of brown liquid. "Oh, that's from Don, our other roommate. He likes to chew tobacco."

So much for trying to make a healthy, new start.

A few nights later, I lounged in Eric's cracked leather chair and gazed around happily. Our room was stuffed with people, the result of an impromptu party. The fermented smell of apple cider and bourbon, a combination known as apple smashers, wafted through the room. I had a perfect buzz going, a feeling conjured from a combination of bong hits, apple smashers, and the knowledge that since the party was coming to me, I didn't have to move. *This is exactly what I was hoping college would be like,* I thought to myself. *No more lonely nights in the Castle.* I felt a looseness, a sense of abandon that was new to me.

A red-headed girl leaned on the edge of the chair. She was short and stocky, kind of like a spark plug, and I could see the outline of her breasts through her tight Oregon Ducks T-shirt.

"Hello," I said. "Welcome to our room."

"So this is your room," she replied. "Quite a party going on."

"You sure are a long way from home," I said, gesturing toward her T-shirt.

"I'm from Portland," she replied. "It's kind of weird to be here. It seems so different than the West Coast."

"I'm from the West Coast too. San Francisco."

She looked genuinely surprised, "No way."

"Would you like another apple smasher?" I asked, recalling that it was supposed to be good to encourage girls to drink more.

Then I was seized by an absurd thought. "I just remembered that I have to put my clothes in the drier. Will you still be here when I get back?"

She gave me a long look. "I could go with you if you want."

The next thing I knew, Alice and I were kissing passionately in the dark laundry room, accompanied by the sound of drying socks. In the past, I had gone so far as to put my arm around a girl, kiss her, and even stick my tongue in her mouth. The rest of my sexual knowledge came from movies, ZAP comic books, and my friends' boastful stories, most of which probably weren't true. I viewed my options as limited: stick my hand up her shirt, put my hand down her pants (though I wasn't quite sure what to do), have intercourse. Fortunately or unfortunately, it didn't come to that.

"Why don't we sit outside," she suggested when her mouth must have gotten tired. We made our way to the back door and sat against the brick wall, watching the trees silhouetted against the black sky. An occasional drunken yell tumbled down to us from the dorm windows.

"I never even saw this place until I arrived here a few days ago," she said.

"How did you decide to go here?"

"They sent me a letter while I was in high school. I guess I was sort of recruited." She paused. "It feels so far from home."

She told me that her parents were divorced, her mother had remarried, and her stepfather was a real jerk. "Kind of a broken home," she said.

Me too, I wanted to say. *I'm from a broken home too.* But I had no idea how to begin.

We chatted for about an hour, when she said she had to get back. I offered to walk her to her dorm and we kissed goodnight. *Yes indeed,* I thought. *Things are working out just as I had hoped.* I couldn't believe how easy it all seemed.

There was something more open about Alice that was different from the girls I had known in high school (not that I had known any well). She talked about her family and home life, flaws and all. Everything had not been easy, she admitted. We could talk about books and found many writers that we liked in common: Kurt Vonnegut, F. Scott Fitzgerald. She read poetry, which in my eyes was romantic and cool. I had an instinctive feeling that she would be able to understand and appreciate me for who I was. Thoughts of her soon filled every nook and cranny in my mind.

For the first couple of weeks, Alice seemed happy to see me when I dropped in at her dorm. On my way home from class or an errand, I anticipated the black scrawl on my white message board to indicate she had stopped by. Often it was there. Accompanied by a friend, she came to watch when I started my first Junior Varsity soccer game at goalie. Then we went to a movie at the Dartmouth Film Society. I had no experience with having a girlfriend or how relationships were supposed to work; nevertheless, I assumed we were in one. I gave her the tiniest glimpses of my life back home, telling her about Helen and the Castle.

And then, after a few weeks, I could feel Alice slipping away. It was a subtle thing, no outward break, just the gradual diminishment in the number of messages, a slight coolness in the way she greeted me when I showed up unannounced in her dorm room. I could tell it was happening, but I had no idea how to change its course.

The less I saw of Alice, the more she invaded my mind. I was tortured by her proximity, just across the College Green, a ten-minute walk from my room. Though I knew intellectually that she cared for me less than I did her, I still stopped by once or twice a week, humiliated by my inability to stay away. One evening after dinner, I walked into her room to find her talking with Chris, a handsome freshman, who was leaning back confidently in a chair. Inside I knew, the way that people hopelessly in love always know, that Alice and Chris were a couple, even if they hadn't realized it themselves. I wanted to escape, particularly after learning that Chris lived one floor up in Alice's coed dorm, but I forced myself to stay long enough to show I didn't care; I was only a friend coming by to say hello. That night I slipped into the bathroom to smoke cigarettes on the floor, an old habit showing its face.

Failure. The word slipped into my mind quietly, almost unnoticeably. Once there, it found fertile soil and began to grow. All through high school, no matter how many times I stared at my eyes in the mirror searching for signs of insanity, no matter how many days and nights I huddled on the bathroom floor smoking marijuana and cigarettes, no matter how many times I watched Mom come and go from the hospital or how many hours of silence I endured with Dad, there was always something to look forward to, something for which to hope. Like a man betting his last dollar on a horse race, I had invested everything in college. Now my horse was falling farther and farther behind.

~

The Bohemian sloth of my dorm room, at first so liberating, began to grate. Dirty socks, underwear, and T-shirts sprouted everywhere like weeds. Plastic cups with Dartmouth stenciled on the side littered the room, some half-filled with stale-smelling beer, and the rest containing a black-brown combination of Don's spittle and Skoal tobacco. At least one of these was knocked over each day, leaving a rancid odor. Not wanting to be a nag or admit I had grown up with Helen to pick up my things, I didn't say a word even as I found it increasingly uncomfortable.

I also began to compare myself to the other freshman guys in the dorm. There was Bob, the star football player, who had been his high school's homecoming king and had a girlfriend back home; Nick, the hockey player, who had already hooked up with a blonde from the dorm next door; Ted, recruited for the crew team, who displayed unbounded confidence with women, even when rebuffed; Sam, an expert sailor and skier, whose easygoing charm and kindness I envied.

I could hang with these guys on the surface, tell jokes, smoke pot, and drink beer. But they had a whole infrastructure behind them: normal families, high school academic and athletic success, past or current girlfriends, confidence in their future. I, on the other hand, had nothing to add when the conversation turned to high school, home, or previous relationships. When Ted, who lived in Palo Alto, mentioned getting together over Christmas, I could only think that he would discover all my secrets: living in a Castle, Helen, Mom's strange illness.

~

I boarded a Greyhound bus to visit a high-school friend at Hampshire College in Massachusetts. During the three-hour ride, I stared at dirty snow and trees with only a few withered leaves on the branches. Everything was tattered, drained of color, bleak. *I could just walk out into that landscape and disappear*, I thought to myself. *Who would know?* Instead of chilling me, the thought evoked the vague outline of a kind-of hope.

My friend and I had known each other since sixth grade, having attended the same elementary and high schools. I had traveled with him to Los Angeles and Mexico, knew his parents, and had spent countless afternoons with him and other friends smoking pot and shooting the breeze. If there was anyone I could share my fears with, it was him.

We talked instead of superficial things: the classes we were taking, Grateful Dead concerts, old friends. I felt this huge gap, as if he and I were on opposite sides of a canyon. I wanted to join him, to cross over, but I had no idea how to lay the first cornerstone of a bridge. How could I just blurt out, "I'm feeling so bad that I would like to disappear?" Or, "My whole life feels like a failure and I don't know what to do?"

I used all my energy to hold myself together, even as the fog began to take over. I found it harder and harder to get myself to class. It was easier to sit on the bathroom floor and smoke. Each week I lied to Mom and Dad on the phone. "Things are fine. Everything is going well."

Everyone began to talk about plans for Christmas vacation. When I pictured my vacation, I didn't imagine myself skiing, trying to get laid, or partying with high school friends. Instead, there I was listening to Mom and Helen bicker, watching Mom play with her food, pretending to everyone that college was going well. Thinking about it made me overwhelmingly tired.

On the plane ride from Boston to San Francisco, I observed the bank of clouds below. *It wouldn't be so bad if the plane crashed*. It actually seemed like a good solution. But of course it didn't. Mom and Dad were waiting in the gate area. I smiled weakly.

"Do you have your return ticket?" Dad asked.

I realized I had left it in the seat pocket of the plane. *What a fucking idiot*, I thought as I walked back onto the plane where the ground crew was cleaning up the cabin. On the way home, while Mom gossiped about parties they had attended and the doings of family friends, I stared out the window and tried to keep myself from crying.

~

Back in the Castle, I felt as if I was trapped. Everything was dark, enclosed, foggy. It took all my energy to get out of bed, into the shower, and dressed for the day. By the time I accomplished these steps, I could only sit at the kitchen table and leaf distractedly through the newspaper.

One day I just blurted it out. "I'm not doing very well... I feel really bad... I'm not sure how to describe it."

Mom came over and sat across from me, fixing me with her blue eyes. "How long have you felt this way?"

"It got really bad this fall at school. I don't know what to do. I'm scared."

She reached out and put her hand on top of mine.

"Oh honey, I'm so sorry. We should talk about this with Dad when he gets home. It might be a good idea for you to talk to a therapist."

"A psychiatrist?" The mere mouthing of the word signaled defeat. Even while fearing that I might be going crazy, the fact that I had never been to a shrink had shored up my vision of myself, an escapee of the Castle.

"I was thinking about Bob Greenstein," Mom continued. Dad and I have seen him a few times for couples counseling and he's terrific. I think he would be good for you."

I sat there, silent.

"Don't worry," Mom said, leaning toward me. "I know what it's like to be depressed." And then, almost as an afterthought: "And now you have some idea of what it's like for me."

~

Bob Greenstein, who'd now seen most of the members of my family, fixed me with an intense, yet sympathetic look.

"Am I supposed to say something?" I asked.

"Is there something you want to say?"

"I'm not sure how this is supposed to work."

"I like to let you steer the conversation. I'm here to talk about whatever you want."

I shifted back and forth in my chair, thinking of those long car rides with Dad when neither of us had anything to say. It was all I could do not to curl into the fetal position.

"I don't know," I finally blurted, "I just feel really, really bad."

"What does it feel like?"

"Like I'm walking around in this dark cloud, and I can't see more than a few feet in front of me. I can barely get out of bed in the morning. And it feels like it's never going to get better."

"How long have you felt like this?"

"A long time. But only recently this bad. It started when I went off to college."

Bob stared at me so intently that I looked at the carpet to avoid his eyes. "I know your parents," he said. "Frankly, given your family situation, it would be hard not to feel bad."

I suddenly found it difficult to say anything without crying. I took a few deep breaths. "You know about my mom?"

"I know all about your mom. And your dad too. To be honest, I'm amazed that you've done as well as you have. I'm not sure I could have managed nearly as well."

I tried to let his words sink inside.

During our second session he asked, "What is your relationship like with your father?"

I was surprised that he would want to discuss Dad, given that Mom was the problem person in our family.

"I feel like I'm always disappointing him, like somehow I'm not a good son."

"Why do you feel that way?"

I told him about coming home from Great Britain after my first year in high school and how Dad seemed angry that I had only written two letters.

"Did you ever consider that it might be the healthiest thing in the world to try and forget about your parents?"

I met his eyes for a moment, then looked away.

"Every 14-year-old wants to escape their parents. That's natural. But in your case, maybe putting them out of your mind was an act of self-preservation."

"What do you mean?"

"If I were you, I would want to get as far away from home as possible too. Your Mom has this strange illness around food and is always going off to the hospital. Your Dad is miserable trying to cope with it. You're stuck right in the middle. Of course you want to escape. Who wouldn't?"

He continued to stare at me, but this time I returned his gaze. I was so grateful for what he was saying that I didn't want to look away.

"You know," he continued, "for various reasons, your parents are both very unhappy. And one of the choices you're going to have to make in your life is whether to allow yourself to be happier than they are. This is not an easy thing to do. In fact, it's incredibly hard. But at some point you're going to have to give yourself permission to feel better than them. It may seem disloyal, but it's something you're going to have to do."

I tried to let his words wash over me, but my mind reacted instantly. *Even if I wanted to make such a choice, how would I do it? It's not like something you can just decide.* I pictured a spaceship trying to exit the earth's orbit.

Feeling uncomfortable, I steered the conversation back to Dad. "When he calls me at school, he sometimes asks why he hasn't heard from me in a while. I always end up feeling horribly guilty."

Bob smiled. "Why is it always your obligation to call him?"

"I don't know," I shrugged. "I'm his son. It's my duty."

He continued to smile.

"I have an idea. The next time your Dad says to you, 'How come I haven't heard from you?' you say to him, 'Hey, I've been right here all the time. You can call me anytime you want. I'd love to hear from you.'"

I felt an immediate release of pressure, as if I had just shifted a heavy piece of luggage from one shoulder to the other. I could actually picture myself standing by the phone in my dormitory and saying these words to Dad.

~

Despite meeting with Bob several more times over Christmas break, I still felt trapped in the black cloud. I felt sick at the thought of returning to school, but the idea of not going back was even scarier. I still wanted that image of college as a place to break free. As if in a dream, I said goodbye to California and flew back East.

Stepping off the bus in Hanover, the cold blasted me like a punch in the face. In my own fog, I had forgotten to put on gloves or a hat, and my fingers and ears instantly ached. I could feel my nose hairs prickle as if they were turning to ice. It was hard to take a full breath. The snow squeaked beneath my feet as I hurried to my dorm room, and was greeted by the familiar mess.

That night I couldn't sleep, listening instead to the constant clanking of the radiator. The next morning I could not get out of bed. My roommates asked why I wasn't going to class. "It's OK," I muttered, "I just don't feel well." After they left, I dragged myself to the bathroom, locked the door, and smoked Camel after Camel, lighting each new one from the glowing tip of the last.

It was there, on the bathroom floor, where the idea first took root. *I could get myself to a motel in some tiny New Hampshire town and kill myself.* The thought provided enough relief to get me out of the bathroom, but not enough to leave the room. I remained inside for the next several days, despite my roommates' asking, "Aren't you going to class today?" I assured them I knew what I was doing. Meanwhile, I refined my plan.

~

When you look back over your life, you can probably identify a few key moments, when everything might have turned out different. Had Dad not answered the phone on that bleak January day in 1980 when I was 18 and on the verge of suicide, I might never have had the opportunity to experience the joys, sorrows, laughter, and pain that life has afforded me.

I had continued to lay out a plan for killing myself. I pictured calling for a taxicab and being taken to a motel in some desolate town. There, I would rent a room, take an overdose of sleeping pills, and end my life. I felt bad that someone would have to discover me and that my family would experience anguish, but those concerns were overwhelmed by the possibility of relief from the blackness and hopelessness that enveloped me.

I don't know why I decided to call home. Some survival instinct perhaps, or maybe, in the end, I never would have gone ahead with it anyway.

"Hi Daniel," Dad said. "How's it going?"

"Not very well," I whispered. I was standing in the middle of the dormitory, one of the only times I had left the room in the week since returning to college.

"Do you want to come home?" he asked. Not, "What's the matter?" or "Do you want to talk about it?" or "You can make it."

"Yes," I said. "I want to come home."

9

MEAN DISEASE

The dream remains so vivid that even now, more than 20 years later, I can picture the images as if I saw them last night. Alone, in a prison cell with cement walls and a barred door, I stand in the middle of the floor wondering what horrid things I'd done to end up there. Every detail, the cold steel of the bars and the rough surface of the cement walls stands out in my mind. I anticipate something about to happen, but nothing does. Instead, I realize that the bars of the cell door have a gap at the ceiling, enough room to crawl over and escape. This sparks another thought. I place my hands on the bars of the door and push—it swings wide open.

I step out of the cell into a long, brightly-lit hallway, like a hospital wing. My shoes click against the linoleum floor that seems to go on forever. I discover a small door at the base of the wall. Opening it, I peek through a crawl space, just big enough for me. I wedge myself in, close the door, and wait to be discovered. Nobody ever comes.

~

"What do you think it means?" Bob asked when I told him about the dream a couple of days later. "It seems pretty significant."

I knew that Bob would force me to grapple with the dream, so I had thought about it constantly. "After I realized that nobody was going to come," I continued, "I left my crawlspace and went back into the hallway. An old friend from elementary school was standing there. He asked if I wanted to join him for a Ping-Pong game."

"Ping-Pong?" Bob asked. "Does that resonate anything for you?"

"We have one in the Castle," I answered, thinking about how in the past two months, I had barely set foot out the front door.

The entire trip home, one week into winter quarter, unfolded in a series of colliding images: refusing Mom's offer to fly to Hanover to get me, visiting the offices of various administrators, asking them to sign the different forms so I could leave school in good standing. One woman urged me to stay by telling me, "We have counselors here trained in this kind of thing." I wanted to reply, "Really? Trained to deal with students who want to drag themselves off to a motel and kill themselves?"

I stood at one of those three-sided telephone booths at Boston's Logan Airport. Because of the public nature of Mom's behavior, I had prided myself on a blank mask of equanimity in public. The more combustible the emotions displayed, the more stoic I became. But there, in the middle of the airport amidst thousands of strangers, I crumbled. I cried and cried while Dad listened on the other end of the phone. "Thank you," I choked, when I was finally able to articulate a few words, then, "I'm sorry," then, "thank you" again.

"Just get yourself on the plane," Dad said. "We'll be waiting for you."

Two weeks into being home, I could barely get out of bed. After waking from a fitful sleep, I would lie in the dark with the curtains closed until Helen came in and flooded the room with light. "You still sleepin' boy?" she would ask. "You sleepin' like it's going out of style." Sometimes, I caught her watching me, a puzzled look on her face. I knew she was being gentle; otherwise, she would have accompanied her discovery of me in bed at 10 A.M. with a more typical, "Boy, get your butt out of bed." With all the struggles Helen had dealt with, growing up in the segregated South and hiring herself out as domestic help, it was probably hard to understand what could be wrong with someone as fortunate as me.

For the first month, I only left the Castle on Tuesday and Thursday afternoons for my counseling sessions with Bob. Before one of our first meetings, I stopped at a drugstore and walked up and down the aisle, reading labels on different bottles of sleeping pills.

As if he had read my mind, Bob confronted me: "Have you thought about harming yourself?"

"Yes," I admitted, with a deep sense of shame.

He grabbed a business card and wrote something on the back. "I want you to do me a favor. I want you to promise that before you do anything to yourself, you'll call me at this number. It could be anytime, day or night. Will you promise?"

I promised, still feeling the black, consuming cloud.

My every activity—getting out of bed, showering, dressing, walking downstairs to eat—felt like it was taking place in slow motion. All my energy went into performing these routine tasks. My only escape, which I achieved intermittently, was sleep.

Most days were spent watching television or sitting in my room trying not to think about the wreckage of my life. I refused to call friends, certain they would reject me when they discovered what a failure I had become. The only person I had to talk to was Mom. She encouraged sharing my feelings with her and kept assuring that everything was going to be OK.

Some afternoons I sat in the kitchen and watched Mom go about her activities. She spent much of her time on the phone. Over the course of a few hours she would negotiate with health insurance functionaries, alternately sweet-talk and bully recalcitrant salespeople, and gossip and share advice with friends. For the first time in a long time, I noticed Mom's strengths: her inexhaustible energy and ability to push forward despite her own struggles, her empathy and obvious concern for friends and family.

For many years I had pitied Mom or been embarrassed by her, but as I struggled to keep going despite the blackness, I saw how Mom, despite her challenges, clung to life. She made clear that she *knew* how I felt, that she had felt similarly many times before. I envied her ability to keep going, to never give up.

Most of all, Mom protected me. She had carved out a place where it was OK to feel awful. She not only didn't judge me, but I sensed she was grateful to have an ally, a fellow sufferer.

A counselor who I saw years later, just before Mom's death, suggested that I talk to a psychiatrist about the possibility of taking antidepressant medications. When I met with the psychiatrist, his first question was about the history of depression in our family.

"I'm not sure about depression," I said, "but my Mom has suffered from anorexia nervosa for many years."

"OK," the psychiatrist responded immediately. "That makes you an excellent candidate for antidepressants."

"Why is that?"

"Depression is passed down through families," he said, "and anorexia nervosa is a type of mental illness frequently associated with depression. There is no better predictor of depression in a child than a parent who also suffers from it."

Until then, I had always assumed that the depression was my own fault. The negative view was that it was punishment for my wanton behavior and insufficient loyalty to Mom and Dad. The more positive view was that it was a subconscious attempt to overcome that lack of loyalty by making myself feel as bad as they did. Now, I had to entertain a third possibility: It was nothing more than genes. Though I knew it could never be that simple, I eased up on myself, a baby step in the long walk toward self-acceptance.

~

I finally left the house one evening to see the movie *Ordinary People*. Bob had recommended I watch it; he thought that I might relate to Conrad, the main character. Sure enough, my face burned as images of my life unfolded on the screen. I saw myself in Conrad's haunted eyes and bedraggled appearance. He lived in a large house on a well-manicured parcel with parents who didn't understand him. He had tried to kill himself and went on to visit a Jewish psychiatrist. And he articulated, better than I could, what I felt: "It's like being in a big hole," he said at one point, "and the more you try to get out the farther in you go."

The end of the movie was disappointing. All it took for Conrad to feel better was for him to admit in a shouting session with the Jewish psychiatrist that he felt guilty for his brother's drowning in a sailing accident. Suddenly, everything improved. I felt betrayed, having had no revelation, no single fact to propel me from bleakness to hope. In a way it was cruel to have had Conrad dangled in front of me—a young man about my age who could understand, who embodied, the inexplicable feelings I had—and then have him suddenly propelled toward recovery and a full life. Nevertheless, my alliance with Conrad made me feel less alone.

Another thing happened that served as encouragement. One day, Helen came up to my room and handed me a letter. It was in a pink, legal-sized envelope with a real Band-Aid stuck across an engraved red heart on the front. The return address surprised me: Abbie Styles, Stanford University. Why was Abbie, someone I knew in high school only because she dated a good friend, writing to me?

Even more surprising was the letter's content. Abbie had gotten a message from a mutual friend at Dartmouth that I had left school. She wanted to say hello. And she wanted to share some of the feelings she had had since beginning college: loneliness, disappointment with the quality of some of her teachers and classmates, how in the midst of an awful cold she had left school and returned home for a week uncertain about whether to return. She did return, but understood how fine that line could be.

I read the letter again and again. Abbie, one of the most attractive and successful girls in my high school, understood how I felt. She was even comfortable enough to share her insecurities with me. I wrote her back with gratitude, unable to convey just how important the letter had been.

I was beginning to realize that all of the things of which I was ashamed— our absurdly large house, our housekeeper, my battle with depression, my strangely ill mother—were outside my control.

~

Normally, each counseling session with Bob was accompanied by a sense of defeat, a powerful reminder of failure. Then one night I had the dream in which I'd found myself in prison. I knew that my subconscious was trying to communicate something, so I wrote what I remembered in the dream notebook Bob suggested I keep by my bed. The day after the dream, I walked into his office with a sense of excitement.

Bob stared at me as I described the dream's details, then waited patiently while I floundered for explanations. Only after my voice had trailed off, and it was clear I had nothing more to offer, did he lean forward in his chair and allow the tiniest smile.

"I like to think that all dreams are actually about the dreamer. And this one seems particularly clear." He paused for dramatic effect. "You've put yourself in jail for no reason. You've declared yourself guilty, but have committed no crime."

"Guilty of what?"

"You feel guilty about living your own life. About accepting the possibility that your life might turn out better than your parents'. Somehow, that possibility isn't OK for you."

His words caused a warming sensation in my stomach. Was I mistaken? Was this my *Ordinary People* moment, the explanation that would allow me to shuck off hopelessness like a skin I no longer needed? While real life doesn't unfold like the movies, I would like to say this was my epiphany. That, like Conrad, I suddenly saw my parents' limitations separately from my own.

A few weeks later, when I awoke to what I expected to be another endless, unchanging day, the black cloud had shifted the tiniest bit. It was still there, thick and dark, but it had moved enough to let in a sliver of light.

My first thought was to notice the change. My second thought was that I might be ready to go back to school.

"Are you sure that's what you want to do?" Bob asked on my next visit, his eyebrows lifting a little. "Do you really think you're ready for that?"

"I want to get on with my life. I want to finish what I started."

"Are you sure Dartmouth is the best place for you? What about Reed College in Oregon? It's supposed to be full of depressed people."

We laughed and this eased my anxiety. I had already made up my mind, in that first moment of relief a few days earlier. "Besides," I said, "I'm only going back for the spring quarter. That will put me on the same schedule as the rest of my classmates. Then I can come back in the summer, and we can continue to meet."

I feared Bob might try to change my mind, knowing that he was right to question the decision. I knew that I had only just started to understand the intense pain I had felt for more than five years. Our work was unfinished, although I didn't want to admit this to myself or be challenged on it.

Dad backed my decision right away. I sensed that he, like Helen, still couldn't fathom what was wrong. "You always seemed as if everything was easy," he responded, after I asked him if he had seen anything coming. "Of all you boys, you seemed to have the easiest time of it."

Mom was supportive, but asked if it was OK if she talked to Bob. I agreed, knowing I needed all the help I could get. With each day, my confidence in my decision increased, and I communicated my plans to Dartmouth.

I received a letter stating that I would be required to remain on campus another two consecutive quarters, which meant I had to agree to stay through the summer.

That day, I had lunch with Mom and Dad at a restaurant named, appropriately enough, the Dartmouth Social Club. I don't recall what started the argument, but I do remember rising from the table and crashing out the front door, well before the meal was finished. I ran up the hills of Pacific Heights, past stone mansions that rivaled the Castle in scale. On an empty street, I collapsed on a set of wide cement stairs and cried as hard as I could ever remember. It probably rivaled the bawling fit I had had on the lawn at Menninger that first time I visited Mom. It was as if the feelings I had bottled up over the years flowed out all at once.

Bob once told me that it can be hard to size up depression because it becomes something familiar. Maybe I cried so hard that day because I knew that in returning to Dartmouth I was taking the first step in leaving behind the life I had known so well. My earlier attempt to leave home had been a false step. This time it was the real thing.

~

"I don't know what would have happened if you hadn't been here," I said to Bob during our last session. "You saved my life."

"I think you'll be all right," he said. "I'll always be here if you need me."

We shook hands and I left his office. I never imagined that it would be 12 years before I once again walked into a therapist's office.

Mom and Dad saw me off at the airport. Without me realizing it at the time, much had changed between us over the three previous months. For one thing, we each knew more about each other. Mom and Dad knew that I harbored a deep-seated pain I had never before revealed. Thanks to Bob, I also knew that they had their own difficulties, which were separate from me. Perhaps most important, I knew that they loved me no matter what, even if I was no longer the "perfect" kid who never needed to see a psychiatrist.

Though I was nervous about how I'd be treated upon my return to school, nobody asked about the absence. That was fine with me, given that I didn't know how to explain it anyway. I continued to muffle my loneliness and insecurity with copious amounts of marijuana. But the longer I was away from home, the more I believed that I was becoming my own person, separate from my past and all that lay back in San Francisco.

Perhaps sensing that New Hampshire wasn't far enough away, I got it into my head that I wanted to study abroad. So I signed up to spend the fall and winter quarters of my senior year at the University of London. Mom and Dad were both supportive, particularly Mom, who harbored a deep Anglophile sensibility. She made plans to come visit while I was there.

Remembering our last family visit to France, I had mixed feelings before Mom's visit. But London seemed to bring out the best in her. She stuffed each day full of activities: The British Museum, the Tate Gallery, the National Museum, St. Paul's Church, tickets to the theatre. I thought about Mom's love of all things English. She loved the formality of the country estates, the literary British wit, the famous English stiff upper lip, drinking tea in an ornate hotel lobby in the late afternoon. The restrained British personality seemed a closer fit to her East Coast upbringing than the brasher, wide-open western one.

Mom even seemed easygoing about dining; the British palate of vegetables and unadorned chicken matched her tastes. Since the entrees lacked sauces and unusual combinations, she had no reason to send them back to the kitchen. One of the highest compliments Mom could endow on someone was that they were "plain vanilla—what you see is what you get." England was a country full of people who acted and ate like plain vanilla. No wonder it suited her so well.

When it came time for her to return to San Francisco, I accompanied Mom to Heathrow Airport and waited with her at the gate. "I had such fun," she said, her face crinkling in a smile. "You're so lucky to have a chance to live here, Daniel Boone. Make the most of it." Then she was gone, leaving me with a glimpse of the woman Mom had been and might have remained had it not been for her mean disease.

~

Throughout the four years I spent at Dartmouth, Mom stayed out of the hospital. I might have forgotten about anorexia nervosa had the singer Karen Carpenter not succumbed to the illness in 1983. I had loved the Carpenters' music (something I would have been loath to admit at the time), and songs like "We've Only Just Begun" transported me to what I considered the halcyon days of the early 1970s. More important, the Carpenter's were one of the few groups that bridged the vast musical gap between my parents and me. While even my wildest fantasies could not sustain a vision of Dad turning up the car radio and belting out, *Driving that train, high on cocaine, Casey Jones you'd better watch your speed,* I could imagine him humming along to "Top of the World."

But Karen Carpenter's death meant more than the end of an era. It meant that the words *anorexia nervosa* began to leap out from all kinds of unexpected places: the cover of *People Magazine*, the mouths of talk show hosts, even in a skit on *Saturday Night Live*. The words always jolted me, as if they exposed an x-ray of hidden shame. I hated the harshness of the term, which always evoked a dancing, grinning skeleton from a Grateful Dead album cover.

At the age of 21, I ignored the implications of Karen Carpenter's death. Years later I learned that anorexia nervosa has the highest mortality rate of any mental illness, anywhere from 6 to 15 percent.

In my college graduation snapshot, Mom's cheek is pressed next to Dad's, and her tanned face contrasts with her still-blonde hair. Though her face is thin, she still looks younger than her 54 years.

After the graduation ceremonies, Mom and Dad whisked everyone to the Mount Washington Inn for a few days. One afternoon, I sat alone on the hotel's wooden deck, sipping a Coke, and gazing at the mountain's gray granite which, according to the Dartmouth school song, would remain forever in my muscles and my brain. I chuckled at the thought, since I had recently vowed to limit my marijuana intake specifically to extract some of the rocks from my head.

Through all my years of high school and college, I had basically been stoned. I never thought about it in psychological terms. I only knew that I felt sad and lonely and incredibly insecure about myself and my family. After college, I would gradually move away from marijuana. Though I still loved to get high, I somehow knew that I could no longer live in a prolonged stupor.

Not being stoned all the time does not mean that one is instantly alert. Habits of mind such as inquiry and exploration, so long subdued, do not come back right away. More than one psychologist has told me that smoking pot retards development. If this is the case, then by the time I was 22 and finished with college, I was also in many ways still the 14-year-old kid who first discovered the excitement and release of marijuana.

Although I had lived in the Castle all of those years, I felt particularly relieved when Mom and Dad announced that they had decided to purchase a new house and were selling the Castle. The new house, a Victorian on Union Street, required extensive renovation; in the meantime, they would be moving to a small apartment in a complex near San Francisco's City Hall. Although I had lived in the Castle for all but six of my 22 years, my only reaction was relief, as if a large weight had been cut loose from my legs. To this day, though I still marvel that I ever lived in such a house, I can conjure no emotional connection to it. In my memories, it is heavy and oppressive, pressing down on all of us. Its removal from our lives promised a sense of relief, particularly, I hoped, for Mom.

Mom had not been in the hospital since I first left for college. And given her mood when she visited me in London and then at graduation, it seemed as if life was finally settling into a routine. "This is the way it should be," one of Mom's friends said to me. "This is the time in life when your parents are supposed to be sitting by the fireplace knitting and reminiscing while you go out and forge your own life."

For better or for worse, I became hopeful.

10

EARTHQUAKE

"Your mother suffered a small heart attack," Dad said over the phone. "The doctors are recommending triple-bypass surgery."

"Should I come home?" I asked.

"There's nothing for you to do here. I would sit tight."

I was 23 and it was the summer of 1985. I spent the day of Mom's surgery at my first real job as a Legislative Assistant to Congresswoman Barbara Boxer in Washington, D.C. Instead of thinking about work, I daydreamed back to the second grade when I had also been waiting to hear how Mom had come through a surgery. The doctors had discovered a lump in her chest, and Dad told us that if the surgery didn't go well, she might have to lose one of her breasts. I was too young to understand cancer, but I knew losing a breast was not a good thing. Even before the headmaster had slipped into my music class and asked to see me outside, I had a premonition that Mom had pulled through. Sure enough, his somber expression changed into a smile.

"Your mother is fine," he said. "They didn't have to remove anything."

From that moment on, I believed that Mom was indestructible. None of it mattered: the repeated hospitalizations, the countless dental procedures. She was a survivor. She would always bounce back. I could see it in her eyes, a determination to cling to life no matter what. So though the bypass operation made me nervous—after all, anything can happen during surgery—I was not surprised when Dad called late in the afternoon to say that everything had gone fine. What unnerved me was the shaky tone in his voice.

"Are you OK?" I asked.

He paused. "After the surgery, I went to see Mom in the recovery room. It was terrible. She was lying there completely white, no color in her face, with all these tubes sticking out everywhere and for a moment I thought: She's dead, she didn't make it. I'm glad you weren't here to witness it. It really shook me up."

Because of my continuing ignorance about Mom's illness, I had no way of knowing that anorexia nervosa often leads to cardiac disturbances, one of the many examples of the illness's destructive power. For me, the heart attack was just another example of Mom's horrible luck. It was harsh that she had to endure such things, but I had no doubt she would survive.

~

Although my time in Washington D.C. had helped to harden my carapace of independence—I had purchased a used Ford Fiesta with my first paycheck and rented a house with four friends—I was about to discover whether it was thick enough to withstand another full frontal assault.

The phone rang on a hazy Saturday morning. After a party the night before, the house smelled of stale beer and humidity.

"Good morning," Dad said, his voice distant and strained. "How's everything?"

"Fine," I said, feeling a needle of pain in my head. "Still trying to do the nation's business."

"Good, good. Listen, I don't know how to say this, so I'll just come right out with it." He paused. "Your mother and I are separating."

I groped for something to say as Dad, who had been right next to my ear, receded down the phone line as if at the wrong end of a telescope. His words were oddly familiar. I had in the past considered the possibility of a divorce, once even flipping through my elementary school yearbook and counting the number of my classmates' parents who were still married. Mom and Dad were in the minority.

"Is the decision mutual?" I asked. In retrospect, I might have asked why this was happening. But I guess, at some level, I already knew the answer.

"It's pretty much my decision," he answered.

"How is Mom doing?"

"I think she's OK, but that's something you'll have to talk about with her."

"Are you moving out?"

"I've taken an apartment on California Street, near the Fairmont Hotel."

And then Dad had to rescue me; I had run out of lines.

"Listen, I'm coming to New York in a couple of weeks. Why don't you come up and we can talk about it more, in person. I think that would be better."

"OK," I said. "That sounds like a good plan."

On the phone, Mom's voice was composed and soothing. "It's only a separation. It has to do with my operation. When your father saw me in the recovery room, I think he thought I was going to die. It scared him, made him come face-to-face with his own mortality. It's caused him to reassess everything. I think it's just temporary."

Like the small earthquakes that rattled San Francisco when I was growing up, I knew something significant had occurred. "Was that the big one?" I used to ask myself, bolting upright in bed and eyeing the plants swinging in their baskets. Without turning the radio or television on, there was no way to know. Mom's reassurance had been the first report from the field, an indication that nothing had been irreparably broken, that the edifice of the marriage was still standing.

~

The Monday after Dad called to announce the separation, I walked into the office and sought out Congresswoman Boxer's Chief of Staff. I found him, as usual, hidden behind a large stack of papers on his desk. He had the look of someone who was desperately seeking to stay afloat despite being drowned in work. Yet he always made time for me. When I asked to speak with him, he ushered me into the congresswoman's private office where photographs of liberal icons like Robert Kennedy and Tip O'Neill decorated the walls.

We sat on the couch. I was suddenly embarrassed that I had chosen to involve him in such a personal matter. But I also knew

I needed someone to talk to. "My parents are separating, and I may have to go back to San Francisco. I don't really know what to expect, but I thought I should let you know."

"I'm sorry to hear that," he said. "Of course, do whatever you need."

"It's only a separation at this point," I said. "I don't have any experience with this stuff."

He gazed at me, as if weighing something. "You know, I used to handle a lot of divorce cases when I was a private attorney. And I have to tell you that 90 percent of the time, couples who separated wound up getting divorced."

Assuming a blank face, I tried to show that I was familiar with these statistics. I didn't want to believe it. I thought about all the years that Dad had shown his fierce loyalty to Mom.

"How did you manage?" I asked Dad many years later. "Your wife with some unexplainable illness from which the doctors say she might never recover. I can't imagine getting through an experience like that."

"It was something I inherited from my parents," he said. "Deep down in my heart there is a little ball of strength, and I know it will enable me to get through anything. No matter how bad things got, and they got pretty bad, I never lost hope."

When Mom first went to Menninger, Dad's parents urged him to get a divorce. He refused to consider it. "I was always optimistic that your mother would get better," he told me. "That is what kept me hanging in there for 20 years."

Given the right circumstances, maybe Dad could have opened up and become more of the person who might have helped Mom get better. His manner, sometimes charming, often distant and re-moved, could leave others wondering if they had done something to bring on his disapproval. In retrospect, the perfect husband for Mom would have exuded love and warmth. That was not the man she married.

Because of her illness, Dad had spent more and more of his time enclosed in that little ball of strength, just trying to hang on.

~

Two weeks later I sat across from Dad, watching the broken yellow yokes of my eggs ooze toward the toast. The restaurant's large rectangular windows fronting a busy Manhattan sidewalk were a stark contrast to the frozen tableau Dad and I presented. The clatter of plates and the murmur of other conversations prevented total silence.

"I know you're angry at me," Dad said. "I understand."

How did he know? I had originally anticipated my role as impartial survivor, unsullied by the need to take sides or assess blame in the breakdown of my parents' marriage. Yet within a short time, I had wound up squarely in Mom's camp. I wasn't sure how I ended up there. Maybe it was the instinctive desire to balance out my brothers.

When I had discussed the separation with Jimmy and John, they were both defensive of Dad. "Look, you can't really blame him," John said in his infuriatingly rational manner. "He's put up with her illness all these years. Don't you think you would do the same thing eventually?"

"Frankly, I'm surprised it didn't happen a long time ago," Jimmy added.

I looked at Dad across the table. "Look, I know you've put up with a lot for many years. I don't know how you did it. But why now?"

"I'll tell you why now." Dad took a sip of coffee. "From the time your mother first got sick and went to Menninger, I always believed she would one day get better. Every time she went into the hospital, I thought to myself, 'This is it. This time she's going to get it.' I felt that way both times she went to Menninger. I felt that way every time she went to Stanford."

Dad removed his glasses and rubbed his eyes.

"And your mother always told me she was going to beat her illness. She told me she'd get better, and I always believed her. After the heart attack and the bypass surgery I thought, 'This is it. She's going to see that if she continues to mess around with her eating that she's going to die.' That message was so clear to me.

"A couple of days after she returned from the hospital, the two of us were in the kitchen and I asked whether the heart attack had convinced her that she needed to deal once and for all with her eating problem. Here's what she said: 'The heart attack has nothing to do with my eating. It's a problem I inherited from my family. My cousin Adele died from a massive heart attack when she was 35.'

"And I said to her, 'Carol, don't you see that this is related to your anorexia nervosa?' And she said just shook her head and said the heart attack had nothing to do with that. It was simply the result of bad genes.

"And then I realized: She's never going to change. It would always be the same. I could no longer sit by and watch her destroy herself. I had to get out."

The waitress stopped by the table. "Is everything OK?"

"You have no idea," I wanted to say.

I couldn't argue with Dad; he made perfect sense. Yet I had already staked myself to Mom's defense, and no explanation, no matter how rational, was going to change my mind. With few words, we left the restaurant.

~

I hardly recognized Mom a few weeks later at New York's Kennedy Airport. I was joining her on a trip to Israel with our family's rabbi and his wife. It was the first time I had seen her since the surgery and separation. Her body had shrunk noticeably, and the red sweater and ankle-length denim dress she wore hung loosely from her frame. Her once-clear blue eyes now looked milky, as if washed with glacial melt. For the first time, Mom looked not just diminished, but defeated.

We arrived at our Jerusalem hotel at dinnertime. As soon as the waiter set down the dinner rolls, Mom grabbed one from the basket and began kneading away, as if she were crocheting it. Little mountains of crust began to pile up on her bread plate. I glanced at the rabbi, who appeared hypnotized by Mom's behavior. She grilled the waiter about each entrée: how it was prepared, what were the side dishes, could she have the vegetables steamed instead of sautéed, could the sauce be served on the side or better yet, no sauce at all. Mom handed her menu to the by-then homicidal waiter, picked up her dinner roll, and smiled at the rest of us as if nothing had happened.

After dinner, Mom and I went up to our shared room. She disappeared into the bathroom and didn't emerge for an hour. I read my book and tried to ignore it, but I couldn't concentrate. *What could she possibly be doing in there? What the hell is going on?* She finally emerged with a cheery, "all yours." I walked into the bathroom and immediately smelt something sour. While brushing my teeth, I noticed what looked like little brown pieces of cooked oatmeal sprinkled around the drain. A closer inspection revealed particles of chewed food.

A common misperception about anorexia nervosa is that people with the disorder do not experience hunger. In fact, persistent hunger is one of the reasons anorexics obsess about food. Part of the power they gain is from the denial of food *in spite of* their powerful hunger. In that context, chewing and spitting out food serves two purposes. It allows for the sense and feeling of eating, but it prevents the addition of any unwanted calories. Psychiatrist Hilde Bruch quotes one of her patients: "I chewed up French fries and spit them back onto my plate. I wouldn't swallow them because I knew if I swallowed them I might gain weight."[3]

What did I do with my realization that Mom was chewing and spitting out her food, probably crackers she had pocketed from the dinner table? Did I rebuke her and ask what the hell was going on? Did I put my arms around her and say how sorry I was about everything? Did I call my brothers and seek their opinions? I did none of these things. It was as if someone had clipped my vocal chords, making me unable to speak. I finished brushing my teeth, cleaned out the sink with a piece of toilet paper, and crawled into bed, trying to think about nothing at all.

The unfiltered exposure to Mom was more than I could stand, and after a few days in Israel, I began a mental countdown to the end of the trip. Faced with one of Mom's downward spirals, I wanted to shake her and tell her it was time to shape up—to move on with her life, to quit with the strange behavior, to eat like a normal person. Not being able to say any of this, I drew deeper and deeper inward. I spent my free time burrowed deeply into the book I had brought along, trying not to think about Mom at all.

At the Wailing Wall, the holiest spot for Jewish people, Mom penned a note and placed it in a crack in the blonde stone. Tradition holds that when the Messiah returns to earth, he will read the notes and grant the wishes. I have always wondered what she wrote. Did she wish for Dad to come back? Or was it for the return of her health? Or simply for an end to her pain?

We finally returned to New York and I kissed Mom goodbye before heading off to my gate. I paused to watch her shuffle away. She moved slowly, her body slumped and curved, as if she were bearing some tremendous weight. I imagined her returning home, alone, to a house without Dad. And suddenly my insides felt like hey were being wrung out with a hard twist. All the way to my gate and even once on the plane, I could not stop chastising myself for the anger and embarrassment I had directed toward Mom throughout the trip.

Without realizing it, I had come face-to-face with the most invidious aspect of Mom's illness: It was a no-win situation. After more than 20 years of living with Mom's illness, Dad had concluded that the only solution was to escape. Remaining involved meant continuing to ride an unceasing emotional roller coaster. His presence had always blunted for us the sharpness of those highs and lows. Now that he was no longer involved, my brothers and I had to get firmly on board.

~

Since John and I both lived on the East Coast, we could only lob encouragement over the phone to Jimmy, who helped Mom settle into Woodside Women's Hospital, a new eating disorder clinic that had opened near Palo Alto. By the mid-1980s, thanks in part to Karen Carpenter and increased media attention in general, awareness of anorexia nervosa had spawned numerous eating disorder clinics around the country, and Woodside was one of these programs. How Mom had learned about it, or why she chose to go there, I didn't know. For the first time, I was not surprised by the news of Mom's departure; for the first time, her hospitalization brought me a sense of relief.

But the strain in Jimmy's voice added fuel to my resentment toward Dad, who supplied additional kindling by announcing that he had stared dating someone, another Carole—of all names—whom he had met in a therapy group.

My brothers and I went through the ritual of breaking bread with the new Carole in our lives. She had invited the Becker men to her duplex apartment in the Noe Valley neighborhood for a get-acquainted dinner. On one of their first dates, Dad had taken Carole to a San Francisco steakhouse, and as he later shared, when he saw her tuck into a big, juicy slab of beef, his heart had done a flip-flop. Perhaps hoping to engender a similar reaction from Dad's children, she had invited us over for a steak dinner.

Carole decided to barbecue a steak on a small hibachi on her deck, which meant that we spent most of the evening sitting around the living room getting to know each other. Although I was armed to dislike Carole, I could find little on which to build a case. She was in her late 40s, midway between Dad's age and my own. She had shoulder-length brown hair and brown eyes and a nice smile. I noted that she was neither fat nor thin, her body size distinctly unremarkable.

"It's nice to finally meet you," she said. "I know that this is difficult."

Dad had already let us know that Carole could be disarmingly direct. One night, driving to the opera, the two of them dressed to the nines, Carole had rolled down the passenger window to address a taxi driver who had cut them off. She motioned for the taxi driver to roll down his window.

"Excuse me sir," she said sweetly, "but fuck you."

She then rolled up the window.

While we tried to make small talk, Carole and Dad kept darting out to the deck to check on the meat. "I think she's pretty nervous,"

Jimmy said, and I suddenly realized that I still held some power in the situation, the power to refuse approval. But once again, my brothers had already outflanked me. Jimmy had already met Carole several times and liked her. John was sanguine, happy as long as Dad was happy.

We ended up eating the steak in stages, cutting off pieces as it continued to cook on the hibachi. It was late by the time we finished the meal and said our good nights. On the way home, I could picture Carole collapsing on the couch now that this meeting was finally finished.

"What's she like," Mom asked, when I visited her at the hospital on the eve of my return to Washington. "Is she pretty? I hear she's a lawyer. Is she smart? Don't you think it's weird that her name is Carole?"

"She seems OK," was the best I could muster.

"Does Dad seem happy to you?"

"I don't think this is an easy time for him," I said. "It's difficult for him just like it is for you."

"I still think it's a phase. I think it has to do with my surgery."

Certainly, a new phase was beginning. Mom was in the hospital (where she would remain for close to a year), unwilling or unable to accept the realization that her marriage was finished. Dad, though sorry, was moving on with his new life. My brothers and I were accepting our new job of worrying about Mom.

"Look at it this way," Jimmy said. "She wasn't going to get better living with Dad. Maybe the divorce will makes her change."

"Yeah," John agreed. "This might turn out to be the best thing that could have happened."

~

"What really upsets me," Mom said, the next time I saw her in person, "is that Carole knows all about Dad's and my private lives. And don't you think it's weird that we have the same name?" We were sitting in the Sizzler Restaurant in Redwood City, California, a ten-minute drive from the Woodside Women's Hospital. Mom looked thin and haggard, her cheeks puckered in, the bones pushing out over her face. Despite the anorexia nervosa, she had always looked younger than her age. Now, she looked considerably older than her 57 years.

Woodside did not allow patients to leave the hospital for meals unless accompanied by a family member. Mom seized on our visits to have dinner at the local Sizzler. She liked the salad bar, everything from cottage cheese to green peas, and an array of salad dressings. Not that the abundant choices made any difference. Mom inspected everything but chose little, while I ordered a steak. I looked at the pictures on the wall—black and white photographs of elegant restaurants—and thought of the anxiety I had accumulated in such settings. Watching Mom at the salad bar, no waiters in sight, I wondered why we hadn't started to visit the Sizzler years earlier.

At the table, Mom pushed the food around on her plate, occasionally placing a bit of cottage cheese on her fork, raising it towards her mouth and then replacing it uneaten. Meanwhile, she kept talking.

"I think your father just got scared. Seeing me so close to death in that recovery room made him aware of his own mortality. He's going through some kind of phase." I listened and nodded, though I no longer shared her optimism.

A few nights earlier, Dad and I had discussed the separation. "How do you see things developing?" I asked him.

"You know Daniel, I just don't see myself going back."

Until that moment, I had hoped that Mom and Dad would reconcile. I wanted it selfishly, but I wished it more for Mom. It was obvious that she still loved Dad very much, that she clung to an idea that her life might, in spite of everything, return to the way it had once been. As if she saw an unbroken line reaching back to her happy days in New York, when she and Dad were newlyweds, and she experienced her first true tastes of love and freedom. Since then, she had had many setbacks, and of course, many disappointments with her chosen partner. But her ability to cling to the idea of normalcy—and to avoid seeing clearly how her illness had affected those she loved—was one reason Mom had always been able to plow forward. The separation had shattered this idea of hoped-for normalcy; the divorce would ensure it could never be repaired.

Sitting across from Mom in the Sizzler, serenaded by elevator music, I wondered who was going to break the news that Dad was not coming back. My brothers and I were now her sole caretakers, a job for which I felt completely unprepared.

11

RESIDUE

In 1989, my brothers and I each shifted west. John and I moved back to California, while Jimmy, who had watched over Mom for the previous year, took a job in Tokyo, Japan. Had I known how difficult the next three years would be, I might have stayed on the East Coast. Instead, I took a job with the State Legislature in Sacramento, a hot, flat 90 miles east of San Francisco.

"Your father is trying to steal what's rightfully mine," Mom said one Friday evening in her apartment. After the separation, the new

Union Street house was sold and she had moved back to the apartment where she and Dad had lived during the renovation. "It's that Carole. I know she's advising him." Ever since Mom had discovered that Dad's girlfriend was a family lawyer, she was convinced that Carole was goading him into a tougher negotiating stance. The specifics of the divorce had become the recurring theme of my weekend visits.

I had driven down late that afternoon and arrived in time to catch Helen, who now came to Mom's apartment only a couple of days a week. Her hours were unpredictable, in contrast to the days when I could set my watch by her 10 A.M. entrance at the Castle. She was 62 now and had worked for Mom close to 30 years. She still spent her time cleaning the bathrooms, making up Mom's bed, and fussing in the kitchen, but now she groaned a little when bending over and she sometimes needed a hand lifting things. She and Mom didn't talk much; they worked around each other, like a long-married couple that avoids stepping on each other's toes. Despite its contentiousness, their relationship had outlasted Mom's marriage. I was grateful that Helen was there to keep an eye on Mom. In fact, she was the only one who could talk straight to her. "Mrs. Becker, you ain't eating hardly anything," she might say, or "You getting way too thin."

Though the issue of Mom's anorexia nervosa was no longer hidden—after all, it had been the reason Dad finally left the marriage—it still remained a subject I could not comfortably discuss. It was as if all those years of learning to ignore what was right in front of my face had left me incapable of mouthing the words. The best I could do was make offhand references. Sometimes, when Helen and I were alone, I would ask, "Is Mom eating?" Usually, she would just shake her head and sigh.

I sometimes ask myself why I never confronted Mom about her illness. Not talking about it was a habit my brothers and I had perfected since she first went away to Menninger. It was as natural to us as bathing. Sometimes I wonder if talking about it would have made a difference, but I never felt I had a choice.

"Shall we have Indian food?" Mom asked, as soon as Helen left.

Mom had taken a liking to an Indian restaurant a few blocks from the apartment, and she frequently suggested that we get takeout for dinner.

She liked nibbling the *saag paneer*, a mushy spinach dish infused with pieces of cheese. Mom's teeth had been giving her trouble, and she must have liked the consistency of the dish, so much like baby food.

After we spooned some food onto our plates and sat opposite each other at the kitchen table, the talk turned to the divorce.

"I'm worried," Mom said, poking at her food. "I'm afraid I'm going to wind up poor."

John, who assumed the responsibility for overseeing Mom's finances, had tried to reassure her. However, his words did nothing to assuage her fears.

Mom continued, "I don't understand why your father is acting this way. He's being downright mean."

I couldn't stand being put in the middle of the divorce. The thought whirled through my head: Should I just ask her to stop discussing it? I had tried this on a couple of occasions, but the way she had covered her mouth with her hand and apologized through her fingers made me wish I hadn't said anything. Maybe I should show some sympathy, I thought instead, but I didn't want to. I couldn't deny that part of me took perverse pleasure in denying Mom what I knew she wanted. It was the only way I could retaliate for everything she had put me through: refusing to take care of herself, obsessing with food, the absences from my life.

But no sooner did those thoughts enter my mind than others rose up to crush them. *Don't you understand that she's sick and it's not her fault? How can you be so hardhearted?* I found myself trapped in this cycle of thinking each time the two of us got together.

~

For Mom's 60th birthday, my brothers and I threw a party in her building's banquet room. Though it was a far cry from the Castle, we tried to make it festive by hanging bunting and multicolored balloons on the white walls. Mom made up the guest list and we invited all of her friends. Jimmy was still living in Tokyo and had phoned Mom the day before the party to express his regret for not being there. Then he boarded a plane and flew to San Francisco. After being picked up from the airport, Jimmy hid in the hallway while we told Mom there was a surprise waiting. She closed her eyes and took a seat at the table. When she opened them to see Jimmy with his arms outstretched, she immediately lowered her head. For an agonizing moment, I feared we had induced another heart attack, but she eventually raised her head to reveal tear-stained cheeks. "I don't believe it, I just don't believe it," she repeated.

For the party, Mom wore white silk pants and a Chinese-style, pink silk jacket. Her hair, still blonde, was cut in a short bob and, had she had more flesh, she would have looked remarkable for her age. As it was, the way that clothing hung off her shoulders, she resembled a scarecrow. The guests could see that despite her display of energy, Mom was disappearing.

From the buffet table, I watched Mom circle the room, making small talk with each guest. "Thank you for coming; so nice to see you; how have you been?" She sat for a long time alongside our rabbi, who was himself wasting away from cancer. She leaned close to speak with him, hanging onto the words of someone who had been a dear friend and spiritual mentor. Noting their similarity—both of them gaunt, haggard, literally worn down by suffering—drained much of the event's festivity for me.

The party had the typical elephant shape with a trickle of people at the beginning, the room stuffed with guests by the middle, and a few stragglers at the end to help take down decorations and box up the leftovers. After returning to Mom's apartment, we collapsed on the sofa, basking in the afterglow and relieved that it had gone so well. I was left, however, with a feeling of emptiness, as if something had been missing. I realized what it was exactly two years later when the same group of guests, this time dressed in black suits and dresses, gathered to attend Mom's funeral. The birthday party had not been a celebration Mom's life; it was a prelude to the mourning of her death.

~

After more than 25 years of starving herself, even Mom's remarkable constitution was bound to wear down. Her teeth, which had caused her trouble for such a long time, were finally beyond saving. She was fitted for dentures, which never looked quite right to me. They caused her mouth to jut far over her chin, and the teeth themselves were too white and even. Their presence, though, was nothing compared to their absence. Sometimes when I stayed the night at her apartment, I would come downstairs after dinner and find Mom in bed, reading. When I entered the room and she smiled with bare gums and lisped a greeting, I could not get over the shock that she looked so old.

Of course, there had also been the heart attack. Though she failed to convince Dad, I had heard Mom attribute the problem to her genes so many times that I stopped thinking about it in terms of the anorexia nervosa.

Finally, the curve in Mom's spine was worsening. I later understood that osteoporosis is another symptom of anorexia nervosa. When sitting, her frame began to take on the shape of a question mark. I could see the spine's curve through the back of her blouse or sweater, like a whale bone displayed in a museum of natural history.

What I couldn't see was what was happening inside of Mom. Though it was obvious that she had lost weight since her return from Woodside, I assumed that, like all the times before, it was only a question of needing to eat more. I had no idea that her organs, malnourished and mistreated for so many years, might finally have had enough.

~

Even though I was 27 by the time I returned to California, I still did not know myself—who I was, what I wanted from life, even what I liked to do with my free time. Thus, at the same time Mom was spiraling downhill, I could not direct my full attention to her. It was only later, after she died, that I had the discipline to sit down and read about anorexia nervosa. In retrospect, all the signs—particularly the physical ones—are clear from the literature. But I did not know the literature at the time or even that it existed.

The drum roll for Mom to return to a treatment facility grew steadily as her friends, as well as Helen, mentioned it. Helen had taken over Dad's role of soliciting Mom about her weight, since my brothers and I were uncomfortable discussing it. As the details trickled back to us, Mom responded with a new defense, "What's the point?"

Alarmingly, John seemed resigned to agree with her. "Listen, if she doesn't want to battle it anymore, why should she? You have to admit that she doesn't have much to look forward to, just more of the same." Although I lacked a good response, some combination of optimism and ignorance allowed me to continue to hope. I had learned through experience that it was easier to be shocked by everyone else's lack of feeling rather than look at the situation in the hard light of reality.

Mom's doctor intervened, suggesting that instead of entering a program, she agree to be fed intravenously at a hospital to jumpstart her weight. In healthier times over the past several years, Mom had weighed over 100 pounds. She was now down to only 70 pounds.

She reluctantly agreed to the IV program and began a pattern to be repeated several times over the next few months. Mom would enter the hospital for a few days, her weight would increase thanks to the plastic tube in her arm, she would return home with optimism and purpose, and the weight would then dissolve as fast as she had put it on.

After a few rounds of this approach, she said she no longer wanted to go to the hospital. Instead, we arranged for the feeding to take place at home under the supervision of a nurse. I sat with Mom on one of these occasions, watching the milky fluid flow through the tube into her spindly arm. I never saw the substance as just calories, but as energy. It was not just keeping Mom alive, but reviving her, allowing her internal engine to recharge, kick into gear, and take over. I truly believed that each feeding was going to be the last she would need.

Again, had I known more about anorexia nervosa, I would not have clung to such hope. Despite the evidence in front of my eyes, I still didn't realize, as Hilde Bruch has written, just how deep or intractable the illness can be:

> Through my work with many patients, I have been im-
> pressed that an anorexic's whole life is based on certain
> misconceptions that need to be exposed and corrected
> in therapy. Deep down, every anorexic is convinced
> that basically she is inadequate, low, mediocre, inferior,
> and despised by others. … All her efforts, her striving
> for perfection and excessive thinness, are directed
> toward hiding the fatal flaw of her fundamental
> inadequacy.[4]

I didn't know that an anorexic patient's starvation adds to the psychological problems and, as Bruch writes, "can becloud the underlying issues," nor did I know the extent to which many anorexic patients cling to their illness. As one Stanford doctor explained, "It's the only disease I know about where people like their illness. They do not want to get rid of it."

~

In previous times, Dad only called when he had something to tell me. Now, sometimes I would answer my phone in Sacrmento and it would be Dad on the other end just checking in. One day he called to say simply that he wanted to make sure that the divorce, which was now final, did not drive us apart. "I know," he said, "that I used to rely on your mother to maintain my relationship with you and your brothers. I know that I have to make more of an effort now if we are going to stay in each other's lives." He paused. "I don't want to lose you guys."

I woke early on a Saturday morning and went out to get a newspaper. When I returned, the message light was blinking with a call from Dad. I phoned him back. "Where were you so early on a Saturday morning?" he asked, a sly tone in his voice.

"I just went out to buy the paper."

"That's too bad. I was hoping that maybe you hadn't come home last night."

Our relationship had reached a new state of maturity. We could even joke about sex.

In contrast, my feelings toward Mom often translated into guilt. One weekend I went hiking and camping with a friend in the Sierra Nevada mountains. It was one of the few weekends I hadn't gone down to San Francisco and visited Mom. As soon as we were heading south on Interstate Five, I opened the window, let the wind blow in my face, and reveled in the freedom of the open road, a feeling I had mythologized ever since reading Jack Kerouac's *On the Road* in high school.

But only a few miles into the journey, my mind took an unexpected left turn and began generating haunting images—Mom, alone in the apartment, moping around the kitchen; Mom, in the bookstore at the base of her building, moving up and down the aisles as a way to stave off loneliness. And then, the images' residue: How can I be going off enjoying myself when Mom is home alone, suffering? What kind of a person am I anyway?

If only I could have pulled out and dusted off the question that Bob had lain out for me ten years earlier. *You have to ask yourself,* he had said, *whether you are willing to allow yourself to be happier than your parents.*

At the next gas station, I went to the payphone and placed a call to Mom.

"Hi honey," she answered, "are you off on your trip?"

"Yes." I paused for a moment, trying to think of just what I might say to make myself feel better. "I wanted you to know that I'll be thinking about you this weekend."

"That's nice," she said. "I'll be thinking of you too."

On another weekend I agreed to be Mom's date for a wedding in Atherton, a suburb of Palo Alto. It was a hot day and Mom wore a straw hat, as if attending a garden party in England. Not knowing the bride and groom, I spent the service daydreaming, until Mom's grip on my hand jolted me to the present. The rabbi stood with his arms open like a canopy over the couple, delivering a benediction. I glanced at Mom to find her dabbing her eyes with a handkerchief.

"Are you OK?" I whispered, fighting back the small surge of panic that welled up whenever Mom displayed strong emotion.

She leaned close to my ear, sobbing gently. "I used to really believe in these things the rabbi is saying. But after your father and I divorced, I just can't believe in them anymore. They no longer have any meaning for me." I continued to hold her hand, while Mom wept, not just for the loss of her marriage, but also, it seemed, for the loss of her faith.

~

As with so many portents in my life, the beginning of Mom's end came with a phone call. John was on the other end. "Mom is refusing any more feeding. She says she's tired and doesn't want to do it anymore. Frankly, I think we need to support her. I've called Jimmy and he's coming home for a visit."

The next time I visited her apartment, the IV stand was nowhere to be seen. It had been relegated to the storage closet in the basement.

When I went down to her bedroom, the room smelled slightly sour. I squeezed behind her desk to slide open the glass door and glanced at the courtyard of the apartment complex. The swimming pool, lit up turquoise in the darkness, beckoned. I longed to be in the water, swimming as hard as I could, thrashing my arms and legs. Surely, Mom would find some reason to change her mind, to hang on, to rage against the dying of the light.

~

"Do you think my mom is committing suicide?"

This was the question I posed to my therapist, Jeff Wagner, at his office in Davis, California, a 20-minute drive across brown rice fields from Sacramento. It was my fourth or fifth visit to Jeff, and I was still skeptical of him. He frequently punctuated my soliloquies with clucking sounds, occasionally letting out a full-fledged "Ugh!" after I recounted a painful situation. Bob, the psychiatrist who had helped me at the beginning of college, would never have done that.

"That's a good question," Jeff replied. "It would perhaps be easier for you emotionally if your mom was dying of cancer."

I had returned to therapy for the first time since college, thanks mainly to my girlfriend who had insisted that we try couples counseling after yet another bad fight. I reluctantly agreed, but felt a slight sense of victory when the couples counselor, upon hearing my story, exclaimed his surprise that I had managed as well as I had to date. He suggested that I might benefit from individual counseling.

I was taken aback at his suggestion that I was somehow managing well. My job felt unfulfilling. I hated living in Sacramento. My relationship with my girlfriend had become a series of soul-draining fights. To top it off, I was approaching my 30th birthday, which had forced me to make this terrible accounting in the first place. And above everything else, Mom was quietly fading within the walls of her San Francisco apartment. If ever there was a good time to reinitiate therapy, this was it.

However, the first time I drove to see Jeff, I had to battle a sense of defeat. Deep down, I had known, ever since exiting Bob's office for the last time 12 years earlier, that that I would someday need to return to therapy, to complete the work I had begun. But as time went on, I distanced myself from the experience. Therapy, I again decided, was for the weak of heart. It certainly hadn't done much good in Mom's case. I could recite a whole list of Mom's psychologists and psychiatrists. And what had it all added up to? Mom, at home, ending her life the way she had lived it, by denying herself the nourishment needed to live and be healthy.

Whereas Bob had worn slacks and a jacket, Jeff wore flannel shirts and Birkenstocks. At our first meeting, I told him my story of Mom's eating disorder and what life had been like growing up. When he interrupted me to inject phrases like, "Wow, that must have been hard," or "I can imagine how painful that must have been," I found myself growing annoyed. I don't need compassion, I told myself, I need someone to help me feel better. I couldn't see that the two ideas might be related.

"How was the therapy?" Mom asked, when I reported back after my first visit with Jeff. She had been supportive of my additional counseling and was eager to know how it went.

"A little disappointing," I confessed. "He seems to come from the 'there, there' school of psychology. You know, 'There, there, of course you feel bad.'"

Mom laughed. "Give it a more time."

Despite my misgivings, I continued to visit Jeff until I grew to look forward to our meetings. Although I wished for him to be tougher, to root out the causes of my unhappiness and suggest changes in behavior that would correct everything, there was indeed something soothing in his empathy. Gradually, it began to sink in that perhaps he was right.

My past *had* been painful.

12

EXODUS

Mom approached death with the same meticulousness she brought to life. She and John spent many evenings poring over her finances, getting everything organized. Her desk drawers contained manila file folders stuffed with credit card receipts, bank statements, childhood letters to her parents, yellowing family photographs, old Mother's Day cards. Night after night, John explained the options and documented her decisions: The green cape with the hood to her daughter-in-law Sandra, the collection of handbags to Helen.

When Jimmy arrived for his visit, John thought it would be a good idea if we were all briefed by Mom's doctor. And so, one evening, the four of us—Jimmy, John, John's wife, Sandra, and I—made a semicircle around Mom's bed, waiting for the doctor to arrive. Though Mom was not always in bed, she seemed most comfortable there. She sat propped up by pillows, the queen size mattress seemed to swallow her. Her limp hair and hollow cheeks added to the appearance of sinking. The dentures gave her a somewhat feral look.

And yet, there was no way to deny Mom's happy, radiant demeanor. A blithe spirit permeated the room coming from nowhere. Maybe it was the attention or knowing that her affairs would soon be in impeccable order. Maybe it was relief that any pain was almost over. We heard stories—our grandfather and his wonderful sense of humor, the time I had five jackets awaiting claim in my elementary school's lost and found closet. Mom asked John and Sandra when they were planning to have children. Somehow, it all seemed normal. It was OK to laugh instead of cry, to banter instead of grieve, to act like nothing unusual was happening.

John announced that he wanted to share with us the contents of Mom's will. When he said that we would all inherit some money, I thought back to Dad receiving the large check from his father, stopping at Menninger on the way home, and hearing that Mom might never recover. Yet again, no amount of money could change the situation.

When John began to discuss jewelry, I thought back to when I'd watched Mom in her dressing room. I would hold her diamond ring up to the light to marvel at the sparkling colors. Then I'd run my fingers over the cool, lustrous perfection of her pearl necklace. At the same time I barraged her with questions: "Is this the one Dad gave you? Did this really come from your grandmother?"

Mom's voice snapped me from my reverie. "Sell it," she said, waving her hand. "It didn't bring me happiness and I don't want anyone else using it. Just sell it and split the proceeds."

John jotted a note about the wedding ring. "Any questions?" he asked. The rest of us shook our heads.

I admitted the doctor and escorted him to Mom's room. He placed his black bag on the floor and took his place on the edge of the bed. As he shined a penlight into each of her eyes and made her breathe for his stethoscope, I recognized the scene immediately—it was right out of *General Hospital,* one of Helen's favorite soap operas.

When he finished his examination, the doctor gave Mom a weak smile and asked to speak with us alone. His voice was matter-of-fact, professional. "Since your mother has decided to forego any further IV feeding, she will probably live another couple months at most. At some point, her organs will stop functioning. A common cause of death in these circumstances is heart failure. Just make her as comfortable as possible. And call me if you need anything. I'm so sorry."

~

In spite of the death sentence that hung over Mom, life went along almost as normal. With no guidance on how to behave in such an odd situation, I plowed ahead, though it became difficult. Desperate to find a job closer to home, I applied to be the director of a river protection campaign and drove to Berkeley for a second interview. The board of directors had narrowed the search to one other person and me, and when I arrived for the meeting, they were still interviewing the other candidate. They asked me to return in 30 minutes. I wandered down the street into a used bookstore where I found myself standing before the self-help section. I passed the time thumbing through Elizabeth Kubler-Ross's *On Death and Dying*.

A week later, the chairman of the organization's board called to say they had offered the job to the other candidate.

"Was there anything I could have done better in the interview?" I asked.

"Next time, try to project a little more confidence," he suggested.

Even if I tried to act like everything was normal, my worries about Mom were leaking out everywhere. I did not know how to explain what was happening to anyone other than Jeff, my girlfriend, and my family. In searching for a way to describe the situation, I had posed the question to Jeff about whether Mom was committing suicide.

His cancer analogy was a useful way to frame the dilemma. If Mom had some recognizable physical ailment, at least people would know how to react. But there was no obvious analogy for someone who is starving themself to death, at least none that I knew. This, in turn, led to another question that had been bothering me.

"Do you think she has any control over her illness?"

Jeff eyed me for a moment with a sad look. "I know," he said, "that this is an important question for you."

My conflicting feelings during visits with Mom always zigzagged between anger and guilt. The anger, which I first noticed on our trip to Israel, sprouted from Mom's unwillingness to get better, to "pull herself up by her bootstraps," as Grandma B. might have said. I felt it most when I watched Mom push the food around on her plate or listened to her chatter about restaurants and recipes. Only by forcing the anger deep into my stomach could I prevent myself from spitting it out into the open.

But as soon as I left Mom's apartment, even before the elevator reached the lobby, whatever anger I held in my gut dissolved. It was replaced with a stream of guilt, like venom from a snakebite. *How could I be so unsympathetic? Why can't I be more patient with her?* These thoughts would claw at me throughout the hour-and-a-half drive back to Sacramento.

Desperate to release myself from these extremes, I asked Jeff for his opinion on whether Mom was a conspirator in or victim of her anorexia nervosa.

He stroked his beard for what seemed a long while before he finally spoke. "You know, I'm no expert on eating disorders. My guess is that even if your mom had some control over her illness, it's probably so far advanced by now that it's out of her hands. The point is," he continued, "there was nothing any of you could have done. I hope you realize that."

"I'll try," I said. "I'll try."

On April 18, 1992, five days after her 62nd birthday, Mom invited myself, Sandra, and a couple from her building to a small Passover seder in her apartment. John was away on business and Jimmy was still in Tokyo.

That day, I left my Sacramento office in mid-afternoon and drove west as quickly as I could to escape the heat that had embraced the Central Valley early that year. When I passed the large sign advertising the now-extinct Nut Tree restaurant and amusement center along Interstate 80, I remembered how we used to stop there for ice cream on drives to Lake Tahoe. As the car descended into the edge of San Francisco Bay, I smelled the damp air that lay over the area like a gray carpet. The hills and buildings of San Francisco, peeking out of the fog, looked particularly unreal.

It was 5 P.M. when Helen greeted me at the door, as did the popping sound of frying oil and the greasy smell of potato pancakes. Not only was Helen a superlative Creole cook, but thanks to Mom and Grandma B., she had also become an impressive Jewish chef. Her matzo balls and potato pancakes rivaled anyone's.

"Your momma's downstairs getting ready," Helen said. "Why don't you go and see her?"

"How's she doing?" I asked.

Helen shook her head and I noticed the bags under her eyes. Perhaps because of the brittle nature of their relationship, I hadn't considered the impact Mom's death might have on Helen. She was not much older than Mom, having just celebrated her 65th birthday, and Mom had provided a pension so she didn't need to work anymore. Something else brought her to Mom's apartment twice a week. Habit? Loyalty? Although she had many interests—a garden patch in the Fillmore District, church, her daughters—I also knew that, like the rest of us, she would be cast adrift by Mom's death.

I went downstairs, sidestepping the electric chair that was installed a few months earlier. With Mom's weakened body, she could no longer make it up the stairs, and the chair helped her move between the bedroom and kitchen. A nurse was now in Mom's apartment day and night. "She's in the bathroom," the nurse said, and I stepped back into the hall and poked my head into the bathroom. I found Mom sitting in front of the mirror, applying mascara. Gazing at her, I was seized by an image from childhood, from Edith Hamilton's *Big Book of Greek Mythology*, which I used to find so enchanting. I recalled the story of Eos, Goddess of the Dawn, who fell love with a human, Tithonus, and asked Zeus to grant him immortality. Unfortunately, Eos forgot to include eternal youth as part of the deal, and although

Tithonus continued to live, his body shriveled, his hair whitened, and eventually he lost the use of his limbs. Taking pity on her lover, Eos transformed him into a grasshopper.

Mom had become Tithonus with her distorted features—a death mask on her face, a protruding skull barely covered by skin, her blue eyes dulled like a worn marble, which now burned with a strange intensity, a kind-of madness. Her dentures were on the dressing table like a pair of wind-up chattering teeth as she gummed a greeting, "Hello Daniel Boone."

I kissed her on the forehead and we spoke a little until the doorbell rang.

"Go see who it is," she ordered. "I'll be up in a minute."

Mom's friends arrived at the same time as Sandra. I ushered them in, took their coats, and led them to sit in the living room before I realized we were speaking in hushed tones, as if at synagogue, or a wake. The sudden rumbling of the electric chair portended Mom's arrival and for some reason, everyone stood as she appeared.

I went over to help Mom unstrap the safety belt. She was dressed in the same outfit she had worn for her 60th birthday—white pants and pink silk jacket. In the face of the abyss, she retained her sense of style.

The Passover seders that we celebrated at the Castle were as much about food and friendship as religion. Mom had focused on how the table looked, the consistency of the matzo balls, and the order in which to serve the meal. The religious part was handled by Dad who read the Haggadah, which recounts the story of the Jews' flight from Egypt and eventual settlement in Israel.

The term Passover refers to the Angel of Death, dispatched by God to smite all first-born Egyptian males in retaliation for the Egyptian Pharaoh's refusal to free the Jewish people from enslavement. The night before the Angel's visit, the Jewish families were instructed to paint an X in lamb's blood on their doors, so the Angel of Death would know to pass over these homes and spare the Jews the Egyptians' terrible fate.

It was hard to focus on the meaning of the tale amidst the Castle's opulence, but on this particular night in Mom's apartment, the service took on an Old Testament feel. It was as if we were there, among the Jewish people wandering in the Sinai Desert, waiting for orders from God on how to proceed.

Mom fit the role of prophet. There was a strange luminosity in her eyes, as if she had seen something fantastic that had been obscured from the rest of us. She was fixated on getting the service underway, even to the exclusion of social niceties. If there was a defining characteristic of Mom, apart from her anorexia nervosa, it was her graciousness, and for Mom, being gracious included hors d'oeuvres and small talk before dinner.

Sandra and I were, therefore, surprised when Mom rose from her chair and immediately ushered everyone to the dinner table. "We need to get on with it," she exclaimed, as everyone assumed their seats.

Mom motioned to the nurse who had accompanied her upstairs. "You too, you too," she ordered.

Startled, the nurse walked over and took a place at the table. Looking a little startled herself, Helen, who was listening through the opening between the kitchen and small dining room, appeared with a place mat and silverware for the final guest.

One of the precepts of the seder is to tell the story of the Jews' exodus from Egypt so that it will make sense to everyone in attendance. The nurse's presence provided Mom a perfect excuse to explain each step of the ceremony.

"First, we say the prayer over the candles," Mom said and then turned to the nurse. "We do this at all Jewish ceremonies. Sandra, you light the candles."

At one point, I began to recount something about the seders we used to have in the Castle when I was a child. Mom interrupted me.

"We need to get on with it," she said, gently but firmly. I swallowed my surprise and stole a quick glance at Sandra to see whether she had picked up on Mom's uncharacteristic behavior.

Mom pointed to the seder plate in the middle of the table, upon which sat a lamb shank, a hard-boiled egg, horseradish, a scoop of chopped up apples and cinnamon known as Horoses, and sprigs of parsley. Mom asked me to hold up each one while she explained its meaning.

When she got to the parsley, Mom instructed everyone to pick up the sprig that had been placed on our plates.

"Now," Mom said, turning again toward the nurse, "the parsley reminds us that Passover takes place in the spring. Everyone go ahead and eat some."

Helen piped up from the kitchen. "Mrs. Becker, you know you're supposed to dip the parsley in salt water before you eat it. That's why everyone has a little bowl of salt water at their place."

After more than 30 years of helping Mom organize her Passovers, Helen had become a Jewish scholar.

I braced myself for Mom's angry retort, but it never came.

"Yes, yes, thank you Helen. Dip your parsley in the saltwater everyone; that's what we do."

We made it through the seder, then dined, as we had many times before, on beef brisket, roasted potatoes, and green beans. Mom orchestrated much of the event, but I cannot recall if she ate any food. I doubt it. Once we finished retelling the story of the

Exodus, Mom relaxed, content that she had accomplished her duty. There was conversation, even laughter. At one point, I even forgot that this wasn't just any evening; that the Angel of Death hovered in the corner.

After Mom's friends and Helen departed, Sandra and I helped the nurse place Mom in bed under the white sheets with the tangerine borders. With the covers drawn up to her neck, all that was visible was her tiny head. She lay on her right side, fixing me with her eyes as I gave her a kiss on the cheek and said good night.

"Thank you for a lovely seder," I said.

She smiled faintly. "It was nice, wasn't it?"

Those were the last words we ever exchanged.

$$\sim$$

Since Dad and Carole were away visiting Jimmy in Japan, and the nurse had taken over my customary room in Mom's apartment, I spent that night at Dad and Carole's. The telephone woke me at 8:30 the next morning. It was Sandra.

"The nurse called to say that your mother's in a coma. I'm heading over there now. I think this is it."

"I'll be there in a few minutes," I said. As if in a dream, I dressed and drove over.

Sandra greeted me at the door. "The doctor's here. He's downstairs."

The doctor was bending over Mom, taking her pulse. As he stood and moved aside, I saw that she was lying on her back, her eyes open but unseeing, her face rigid, her breath audible but shallow.

"She'll probably die within a few hours," the doctor said. "I'm sorry. I know its been a long struggle."

He packed up his bag, took a long look at Mom, and started to exit the room. I had my first wave of panic.

"Wait," I said. "What do we do now?"

"You should probably decide what you want to do with her body and start making arrangements."

Because I had never truly believed that Mom would die, I was in many ways unprepared for this moment. In all of Mom's planning, she had failed to say what she wanted done with her body. Cremation made perfect sense. Mom had spent the last 30 years ravaging her own body. She had starved it, cursed it, criticized it, hated it. In the end, she had destroyed it. The last thing she would want would be to spend eternity with it.

I left the room and started making phone calls. Sandra and I remembered that one of Mom's friends had recently had her husband cremated by the Neptune Society. When I called the operator, he told me to phone back after Mom had died and they would come and take the body.

"By the way," he added, "since this is an apartment complex, you might want to figure out how we should plan to enter and exit. Usually, they don't want us going out the front door; it can be upsetting for the other tenants."

I ran downstairs to consult with the black-suited man at the front desk.

"I'm so sorry," he said. "She seemed like a very nice woman. It would be best if they entered through the garage and used the service elevator. The more we can limit interaction with the neighbors, the better. You understand."

"Of course," I said, trying to reconcile this odd mixing of the profound with the mundane.

When I reentered the apartment, Sandra was on the phone with

John, who was in Hawaii. She handed the phone over. "Thanks for being there to help take care of everything," he said. "I'll be home on the next flight." I could tell by his voice that the reality of it had shocked him as well.

"I'll call Jimmy," I said, reaching him at four in the morning. Tokyo time. "Sorry to wake you," I said, "but I thought you would want to know."

"No, it's good that you called," he replied through several layers of time zones and sleep. "Sorry I'm not there to help."

"You've done your share," I said. "You were here by yourself all those years when John and I were back east. I feel like we've all done our part."

"Call me back when she dies, OK?"

"OK."

I rested my head in my hands and contemplated what to do next.

"I think this is it," the nurse said, coming upstairs. "This is your chance to say goodbye."

Returning to Mom's bedside, I stood on the right side of the bed and Sandra went to the other side. We each took one of Mom's hands.

In the past, I had pictured this scene in all its details, right down to me standing next to Mom as her life drained away. I had seen myself as the sympathetic hero, playing a starring role in the drama. Yet now that it was actually happening—just as the doctor had assured—it was as unreal as if I were still imagining it. After all, Mom didn't have cancer or AIDS, or some other terminal illness. She had been with us at dinner last night. Even though she looked awful, I simply couldn't believe that she was about to die.

"Goodbye," I whispered. "I love you."

And then, just like that, she was gone. Though she never moved and her expression never changed, it was clear that one moment she was alive and the next she was dead. Something ephemeral had lifted out of the room, her spirit perhaps, and now all that was left on the bed was a body lacking anything of Mom to animate it. She was finally free, I thought, laying her hand gently on the bed. She had finally escaped from her own bondage.

I remembered earlier when she'd wrapped up her affairs. "It was kind of amazing," John had said, his eyes brimming with water, even though he did not easily show emotion. "She leaned back in the bed, closed her eyes and said, 'I'm done.' Just like that, with a big sigh."

"I'm done."

~

We held the funeral at Temple Emanuel a few days later. Jim had returned from Tokyo and the three of us boys sat together with Helen in her black dress. Dad and Carole sat behind us, one row back. The rest of the synagogue was filled with hundreds of friends. After the service was finished, and we had shaken hands with all of the well-wishers, we went back to Mom's apartment and had a little party with plenty to eat. Mom would have wanted that.

Because I was the only one of my brothers who was with Mom when she died, I was forced to make decisions that normally I would have left to Jimmy or John. This gave me a new respectability in their eyes. When I volunteered to help pack up Mom's apartment, they both agreed that I should do it.

The man from the moving company arrived early in the morning. I sat with a clipboard and pen, taking a careful inventory while he wrapped the contents of each cabinet in newspaper: dishes, glasses, silver. We had already distributed the furniture, so what was left were the odds and ends that seem so overwhelming when you pack up a house—not only the dishes, but the files and the little tchotchkes that you don't want to throw away, and likewise don't quite understand why you are saving. Wanting to acquit myself honorably of my responsibility, I recorded in which box each item, no matter how small, had been deposited. Eventually, my inventory totaled seven pages of yellow, legal-sized paper.

Around 5:00 in the afternoon, the moving man sealed the final box and announced that we had finished. After he departed, the only items that remained in the apartment were the kitchen table and a couple of chairs. John had planned to pick these up later in the evening. In the meantime, they stood like lonely soldiers keeping watch over a now-empty realm. I sat in one of the chairs, rested my elbows on the table, and thought about how much of my life had played out in just this position. And then I cried. Great gobs of tears moistened the table, even as I tried to stop them by placing both of my palms over my eyes. For a moment, everything I had been holding in for so long seemed to be flowing out.

Just at that moment, Dad walked in. Knowing that packing up the apartment would be a difficult task, he had asked if he could come over and take me out once I had finished. I was embarrassed by my tears, but could do nothing to stop them. Dad sat in a chair and gazed at me with a pained expression while I continued to sob and sob. When it appeared the flow was starting to abate, he reached over and handed me a handkerchief, which I used to try and clean myself up. He watched me as the crying became snuffles, then just a few hiccoughing gasps.

At that point, there was a moment of silence, like so many moments Dad and I had shared, when I wished that I knew what to say to remove the awkwardness and allow us to be close, like fathers and sons are supposed to be. He was all I had now, apart from my brothers, and I already realized that I needed him now in a way I hadn't anticipated before Mom's death.

Dad broke the silence.

"How about if we go downstairs and I buy you a Coke?"

I smiled sheepishly and nodded, continuing to wipe my eyes.

EPILOGUE

Ten years to the day after Mom's death, I was at the base of Chomolhari, the holiest mountain in the Himalayan kingdom of Bhutan. I had recently turned 40. Following up on a vow to quit my job and travel if I found myself still single, I decided to make a pilgrimage to the last independent Buddhist kingdom. Six months after Mom's death, I had visited the Himalayas in Nepal with Jimmy on his way back from Japan. There was a kind of symmetry in returning to the highest peaks on earth on the tenth anniversary.

As my tripmates and I hiked into a valley hewed between walls of frost-dusted mountains, I thought about the years since Mom's death. After her funeral, I left California for a job in Seattle and I have lived there ever since. I purchased a little house and discovered a group of close and devoted friends. Though I had not yet found a lasting relationship, a few years later I would marry a wonderful woman.

"It's never too late to have a happy childhood," novelist Tom Robbins has said. Over the previous years, I reclaimed much of the joy I missed out on the first time around.

Dad and Carole's marriage turned out to be a happy one and their love spilled over to my brothers and me. Carole was the perfect antidote to the silence we had clung to in family matters. By sheer strength of personality, she forced us to talk about issues that we otherwise would have buried. As a result, our relationships had matured and grown closer. Mom's death also helped each of us realize just how important we were to each other. It's too bad she missed out on playing with John and Sandra's two children, Rachel and Jake, her grandchildren. She would have loved to spoil them.

During this trip into the Himalayas, I talked a lot about families with the guide, a young Bhutanese man named Sanjay. I mentioned to him that it was the tenth anniversary of my mother's death. "We must light the butter candles," he said, referring to the practice of fashioning candles out of yak butter. "I know a holy spot where we can go." According to Bhutanese tradition, the butter candles were said to light the dark pathways the dead must travel.

Several other hikers joined us on the pilgrimage. We climbed slowly into the thin and cold air, each exhale a puff of cloud. We reached a small lake surrounded by rocks. Other than wind, the only sound was the bells from a herd of yaks nearby. Sanjay knelt down and placed the butter candles on a flat rock behind an abandoned hut. He handed me a lighter and cupped the candles so the flame could take hold. After a couple of tries, I managed to ignite the wicks. We all huddled around so they wouldn't go out.

I thought how glad Mom would have been that I was in such a place for this occasion. The surrounding lake and mountains reminded me of how her eyes would light up when she talked about her days of camping, swimming, and canoeing at summer camp. Had she still been alive, she would have been 72, too old for this trip. But maybe we would have traveled somewhere together, where she could have at least gazed out at a beautiful view and finally recognized her own beauty, love, intelligence, and grace staring back.

Notes

1. Werne, J. *Treating Eating Disorders*, San Francisco, CA: Jossey-Bass, 1996.

2. Morton, R. *The Treatise of Consumptions*, 1689, *http://www.helprkids. com//articledatabase/anorexia.htm* (May, 2005).

3., 4. Bruch, H. *Conversations with Anorexics.* New York: Basic Books, Inc., 1988.

Acknowledgments

It would take another whole book to thank everyone who helped me complete this one.

Memoirs can be difficult for families. My dad and brothers were unfailingly supportive, even when I delved into areas that might have caused discomfort. I could never have completed the book without their encouragement. In particular, my dad was always willing to share his memories and answer my questions. In doing so, he gave me a great gift.

I would like to thank my stepmother, Carole Levine, for constant support, helpful critique, and unconditional love.

Many people encouraged me in my writing, in particular: Larry Cheek, Skye Moody, Bob Goldstein, Steve Nicholas, Harold Taw, Laura Lynn Dixon, Betsy Herring, Michelle Furtado, Carla Saulter, Stacy Bennetts, and Marschel Paul. Nobody could ask for better teachers and fellow writers.

Many people also took the time to share with me their memories or expertise: Dr. C.A. Barnhill, Dr. Jim Ferguson, Dr. JoEllen Werne; Maryanna Shaw, Sharon Bauer, Dr. John Kerner, Prentice Sack, Georganne Conley, Joyce Goldfeder, and Sandra Musser Becker.

One of the happy aspects of writing this book was the chance to meet many of the medical professionals who helped Mom throughout the years. I was so grateful to discover that they were, uniformly, excellent doctors and warm and compassionate people. It was such a relief to realize that Mom was treated by the best. Thank you for all you did for her.

Thanks to Leigh and Lindsey Cohn and Lindsay Woolman of Gürze Books for supporting this book and for their work to help those effected by eating disorders.

Special thanks to Bob Commanday for digging out a key article from the archives of the *San Francisco Chronicle.*

Thanks to Zoka's and Elliott Bay Bookstore for providing space and coffee for lonely Seattle writers.

Finally, I would like to thank my wife, Annette, whom I met in the middle of this project and who, with her love and support, helped me get past the finish line. Nobody could ask for a better partner and friend. I love you very much.

About the Author

Daniel Becker has received Masters degrees from Columbia University and Stanford University. His writing experience includes earning two certificates in nonfiction writing from the University of Washington. His work has been published in *Salon.com* and *Backpacker Magazine*. The first two chapters of *This Mean Disease* earned a finalist spot in the Pacific Northwest Writer's Association's annual literary contest. He and his wife live in Seattle, WA.

About the Publisher

Since 1980, Gürze Books has specialized in quality information on eating disorders recovery, research, education, advocacy, and prevention. Gürze publishes *Eating Disorders Today*, a newsletter for individuals in recovery and their loved ones, the *Eating Disorders Review*, a clinical newsletter for professionals, and the *Health At Every Size* journal. The company also widely distributes free copies of *The Eating Disorders Resource Catalogue*, which includes listings of books, tapes, and other information. Their website (*www.gurze.com*) is an excellent Internet gateway to treatment facilities, associations, basic facts, and other eating disorder websites.

Order at www.bulimia.com
or by phone at 800-756-7533

This Mean Disease is available at bookstores and libraries and may be ordered directly from the Gürze Books website, *www.bulimia.com* or by phone 800-756-7533.

FREE Catalogue

The Eating Disorders Resource Catalogue features books on eating disorders and related topics, including body image, size acceptance, self-esteem, and more. It includes listings of nonprofit associations and treatment facilities, and it is handed out by therapists, educators, and other health care professionals around the world.

www.bulimia.com

Go to this website for additional resources, including many free articles, hundreds of eating disorders books, and links to organizations, treatment facilities, and other websites. Gürze Books has specialized in eating disorders publications and education since 1980.

Eating Disorders Today

A newsletter for individuals in recovery and their loved ones

This compassionate and supportive newsletter combines helpful facts and self-help advice from respected experts in the field of eating disorders. Request a sample issue!